Observation, assessment and planning in the early years

Bringing it all together

Observation, assessment and planning in the early years

Bringing it all together

Kathy Brodie

 Open University Press

Open University Press
McGraw-Hill Education
McGraw-Hill House
Shoppenhangers Road
Maidenhead
Berkshire
England
SL6 2QL

email: enquiries@openup.co.uk
world wide web: www.openup.co.uk

and

Two Penn Plaza, New York, NY 10121-2289, USA

First published 2013

A catalogue record of this book is available from the British Library

ISBN-13: 978-0-33-524670-0 (pb)
ISBN-10: 0335246702
e-ISBN: 978-0-33-524671-7

Library of Congress Cataloging-in-Publication Data
CIP data applied for

Typeset by Aptara, Inc.
Printed and bound by CPI Group (UK) Ltd, Croydon, CR0 4YY

Fictitious names of companies, products, people, characters and/or data that
may be used herein (in case studies or in examples) are not intended to
represent any real individual, company, product or event.

Praise for this Book

"*Observation, Assessment and Planning in the Early Years – Bringing it All Together*, actually does bring it all together. Kathy Brodie has linked theorists from the past to the present, skilfully connecting to the revised EYFS. Early Years students and practitioners will have the opportunity to reflect on the innovative ideas that she has suggested. Kathy has also included detailed information on observing SEN children. This modern update to observation, assessment and planning is a must read for the early years sector."

Laura Henry,
Managing Director, Childcare Consultancy

"This is a very well researched and practical guide to observation, planning and assessment in the Early Years. Kathy has collected together both historical and current thinking and ideas around the subject and then presented them in a way that is easy for the reader to access, understand and, more importantly, apply.

The structure and format of the book helps the reader to check their understanding of the key learning points and then supports them in working through any challenges that they may have along with answers to key questions.

Observation, Planning and Assessment in the Early Years is an essential read for all Early Years Practitioners from those with experience to those just starting out."

Alistair Bryce-Clegg,
Early Years Consultant

"This is a wonderful and timely resource to help practitioners make and use well informed judgements of young children's learning and achievement. The four threads of observation, assessment, next steps and planning are skilfully woven together. Plentiful exemplifications and case studies vividly illustrate theoretical points and give young children a central place in the book."

Marion Dowling,
Early Years Specialist and Vice President of Early Education

Contents

Acknowledgements

I'd like to thank all those practitioners and settings who have encouraged, supported and educated me over the years. Particular thanks go to Des Forrest; Jean Maguire and Vickie Harnley and their team at Goodwood Lodge, Stockport and Catherine Armstrong and her team at Hollywood Park Nursery Centre, Stockport.

I'd also like to thank Fiona Richman at Open University Press for her valuable assistance and steadfast advice, and my family Ian, Chris and Robs whose support has made all this possible.

Abbreviations and acronyms

ADHD	attention deficit and hyperactivity disorder
CPD	continuing professional development
DDA	Disability Discrimination Act
EAL	English as an additional language
ECEC	early childhood education and care
ECM	Every Child Matters
ELG	early learning goals
EPPE	Effective Provision of Pre-School Education (Project)
EYFS	Early Years Foundation Stage
IBP	individual behaviour plan
IEP	individual education plan
PLOD	possible lines of development
REPEY	Researching Effective Pedagogy in the Early Years
SEN	special educational needs
SENCO	special educational needs coordinator
SENDA	Special Educational Needs and Disability Act
ZAD	zone of actual development
ZPD	zone of proximal development

PART ONE

Getting started

1 Background to the early years curriculum

We can be inspired by some whose ideas came – as it were – before their time but yet were not reticent in articulating or realising their ideas.

(Nutbrown et al. 2008: 181)

Chapter objectives

- To consider theorists and how observations have informed their practice
- To explore the legislative and research background of the early years curriculum in England

Chapter overview

In this first chapter I go right back to the beginning of the rich heritage we have of observing children. This has evolved over the years as we try to understand children's thinking and learning, so this chapter contains a selection of key influential theorists from historical and contemporary times. I have highlighted the theorists' different views on observation and methods.

I then go on to examine some of the research and circumstances that have influenced the formation of the Early Years Foundation Stage (EYFS) for England. The current curriculum became statutory in 2008 and was reviewed and revised in 2012, but there are still echoes of the theorists in today's curriculum. Finally some of the terms that are used throughout the book are explained.

Heritage of observing children

Adults have not always observed children and tracked their newly emerging skills. In fact, childhood as a construct is a relatively modern phenomenon, developed in the last few hundred years (Aries 1962). Prior to this children were considered to be small adults and were involved in all aspects of the adult world.

More recently however, there have been many educators who have investigated child development by observing their own children and children in their care. I use the word 'educator' because the theorists discussed here come from a range of backgrounds and disciplines, not just education. For example, Dr Maria Montessori trained as a medical doctor while Jean Piaget was a professor of psychology, sociology and philosophical studies (Pound 2005). The thing they all have in common is that they were interested in how children learn and how knowledge about children's learning may be used to improve young children's lives.

Froebel

Friedrich Froebel was years ahead of his time. It was more than two hundred years ago that he first suggested that the early years were the most important time of a child's life. He was one of the first people to suggest educational toys and to demonstrate the sort of educational uses these may have. Froebel was inspired by Pestalozzi's philosophies, after teaching at a school in Frankfurt that followed Pestalozzi's ideas. In 1839 he opened the Play and Activity Institute, which he later renamed 'kindergarten', meaning 'a garden of children' or 'a garden for children'. At the time, his ideas were considered very liberal and the Prussian government banned his kindergartens. He is probably best known as an advocate for learning through play. He also designed and developed his own educational toys for children in his care, which he called 'gifts', and a series of activities, which he called 'occupations' (Weston 1998).

Froebel believed the role of the adult was to observe the children and understood that the support needed by children in their early years is different to the support required later on. He was very child centred, famously saying, 'a child's play is his work' (Pound 2005) and he was well known for listening to children. Kindergartens are established around the world and his name is still synonymous with play.

Mason

Charlotte Mason was born in 1842 and regarded an education as being essential for all children, regardless of class. She believed it was equally important to inform parents about their children's educational needs and set up the Parents' Educational Union in the late 1800s. Her educational philosophy was that 'education is an atmosphere, a discipline, a life' (Shafer 2007) and she pioneered home education. She was a great believer in children learning through their senses and that a parent's role was to ensure that there were plenty of opportunities for children to be able to do this. A prolific writer, she wrote about educational practices for a range of ages as well as geography books and religion.

She believed that children should be assessed by 'narration' (Mason 1923), which involves children telling others about their learning, either orally or in written or drawn form. The child must be able to understand and synthesize their learning, then be able to communicate this to someone else. This is a high order of understanding required from a child and, in modern day terms, would be described as one of the highest cognitive domains as defined by Bloom (1956).

McMillan

Margaret McMillan worked with her sister, Rachel, in London in the early 1900s. Her particular area of interest was children's basic health and hygiene. She had seen children in Bradford and in London who were suffering from disease and malnutrition. In her book *The Nursery School* ([1919] 2009), McMillan talks of her vision of primary schools welcoming happy and healthy children into their classes, without the 'welter of disease and misery . . . which makes the doctor's service loom bigger than the teacher's' (p. 292).

Her treatment of children and close observations of the effects on them proved that children's health could be improved by simple measures, such as allowing them to sleep outside and play freely in the garden. She wrote and lectured about her experiences, hoping to persuade others about the benefits of outdoor activity, freely taken by children. She would not have been able to make such a strong case for outdoor play without her detailed observations.

Montessori

Observations were the basis of Dr Maria Montessori's interest in child development. She first observed children in asylums and noticed how their development depended on the adults and environment that the children were in (Mooney 2000). In her Casa dei Bambini Montessori observed how the children's development was significantly improved when given appropriate objects to play with. The adults were expected to observe the children and their play at all times. It is from these observations that the Montessori method was formed (Pound 2005).

In modern day Montessori settings, Montessori teachers are still expected to observe children at all times, although the observations must not interfere with the children's work, and particularly not criticize it (Stoll Lillard 2005).

Piaget

Jean Piaget first became interested in how children learn through his work with intelligence tests, where he noticed that there were patterns in the way that children got the answers right and wrong. This made him curious about the way children constructed their knowledge of the world. He made detailed observations of his own three children as they grew up, and the children of his friends. Based on these observations he formed his theory that children develop intellectually and sequentially through four distinct stages – sensorimotor, preoperational, concrete operational and formal operations (Piaget and Inhelder 1969).

However, Piaget's techniques have been criticized because his early observations were centred on his own children and it was felt that there had been no consideration of social learning or context. For example, one of Piaget's tests used mountains (a normal sight in Switzerland, where Piaget lived) but this seemed to confuse other children, not familiar with mountains, who did not seem to understand the task. Once mountains were replaced with barriers however, children did much better on the task (Zastrow and Kirst-Ashman 2010).

Vygotsky

Lev Vygotsky was seen as 'an alternative to the influential concepts of Piaget' (Gindis 1999: 32) because he considered learning to be a social and contextual process. He believed that the observation of children was more important than test scores and that it was essential for teachers to be vigilant observers, so they could better support the children's development and learning. Only by knowing through observation at what level the child is at could the zone of proximal development (ZPD) be established. This information could then be used to plan suitable activities which would challenge and stretch children (Mooney 2000).

Isaacs

Susan Isaacs is considered a modern day pioneer of naturalistic observations. These are observations of children while they play, with no interference or hindrance. The children are allowed to choose their activities freely while the practitioner observes, supports and scaffolds the learning. This, arguably, most accurately reflects the world that children grow up in (Mukherji and Albon 2010). At the school she set up, Malting House School, Isaacs encouraged written observations of everything that the children did or said. In her book *Intellectual Growth in Young Children* she states that accounts should be 'verbatim records and full objective records of what was done should be given' (Isaacs 1930: 1). Although this sounds very familiar to contemporary thinking it was a departure from mainstream thinking at the time; in fact Grenier (2009) believes that any approach that relies on observation based assessment is drawing on the legacy of Susan Isaacs and her beliefs.

Malaguzzi

Loris Malaguzzi developed the pedagogical approach in the village of Reggio Emilia, in Northern Italy, after the Second World War (Edwards et al. 2012). He believed that children should be given the opportunity to express themselves in as many ways as possible. This includes art, drama, 3D models, light and shadows. He called it 'The Hundred Languages of Children'. It is documented through written observations, verbatim transcripts, photos, video, drawings and paintings. Recording and documenting observations made by practitioners is particularly important in this approach, because the representation of the child's thinking may be a short dance or a shadow displayed briefly on the wall.

Hutchin

Vicky Hutchin has written extensively on observing and assessing young children (Hutchin 1999, 2000, 2003, 2007, 2012a). Her later writing is closely linked with the EYFS and gives some useful and practical ideas for using observations effectively in an early years setting. In particular, her book *Tracking Significant Achievement in the Early Years* (2000) has many examples of observations made of children at different ages and their significance for assessment purposes.

Carr

Margaret Carr is best known for her development of learning stories. She describes four processes, where 'describing' (Carr 2001) is the first process and is based on observations. Carr believes that observations should be focussed on credit. That is, the observations should be about what the child *can* do, not what they can't do. She also details how observations should be part of a structure, so practitioners can start to make connections and assess where children are in the domain of learning dispositions, or their attitude to learning (Carr 2001: 123).

Bruce

Tina Bruce describes how practitioners can use observations as a variety of 'lenses through which to tune into and understand the child's development and learning' (Bruce 2005: 204). She also describes how observation can be used to inform themes and the planning of activities for children.

Athey

Chris Athey is closely linked with schema. A schema is a particular way that children explore and examine the world, by making connections between experiences and objects. For example, a box, a drawer and a zoo cage all 'enclose' and will support an 'enclosure' schema. Alternatively, a handbag, a truck and a post van all 'transport' objects and would support a 'transporting' schema. Athey's (1990) definition of a schema is 'patterns of behaviour and thinking in children that exist underneath the surface feature of various contents, contexts and specific experience' (p. 5). Her research during the Froebel Nursery Research Project at the Froebel Institute from 1972 to 1976 (which resulted in the book *Extending Thought in Young Children: A Parent–Teacher Partnership*) is a master class in observations of all descriptions. During this project Athey and her team observed children playing, drawing, making models and interacting and listened closely to the children's explanations for their creations. These were carefully documented and recorded, resulting in over 5000 observations. From these observations the links and connections were made, resulting in the theories of schema learning.

One of the great strengths of this project was that the family was also involved. This included the family in making observations at home of the children's play and discussing this with the Project team. This gave observations context and a rounded view of the child's cognitive development.

Nutbrown

Cathy Nutbrown extended Athey's work on schema in her book *Threads of Thinking* (2006). It also draws on a multitude of practical observations to vividly illustrate points about child development. Nutbrown maintains that 'Adult observation is an essential strand of the curriculum' (Nutbrown 2006: 123) and the method by which practitioners (or educators) can learn about the child's schemas in order to extend them.

Just as Athey does, Nutbrown also uses drawings, emergent writing and story telling in her observations. The exact words and phrases used by the children are recorded, along with their ages, so the reader really gets a feel for the children's play. Without these detailed observations it would be almost impossible to make the links necessary to understand schematic play.

Wall

Kate Wall's area of expertise is children with special needs. She maintains that during observations of children with special needs, their particular condition or need is secondary. The observation should focus on the child's 'current skills, strengths, weaknesses, likes and dislikes' (Wall 2011: 115).

She also believes that observations should be shared with parents, so a holistic picture can be created for each child. It is likely that these sorts of observations will be shared with outside agencies, so may need to be written with other professionals in mind. Wall also highlights the importance of having a clear purpose for the observation, using the appropriate observational methods and being clear on how the outcomes are disseminated.

Comparison of the theorists

From these pioneers we can see how observing children has grown from its early beginnings. Observations first identified children's basic needs and equipment to support their development (Froebel, Montessori, McMillan). They have evolved to underpin the more complex philosophies of children's holistic learning (Piaget, Malaguzzi, Athey). Interestingly, each pioneer has been able to draw different conclusions about how children learn from their own observations. In addition this is linked to their personal experiences, backgrounds and individual methods. For example, Froebel's mother died when he was very young and he only experienced a caring environment ten years later. This affected his views on how children should be cared for. Piaget only used a small sample of select children, but he drew generalized conclusions from his observations (Gray and MacBlain 2012).

Discussion box

Do this experiment with a colleague. Both observe the same child at the same time during a free play activity. It can be indoors or outdoors. Make individual notes in your own style and do not confer during the observation.

After five minutes, compare observations and note the differences and similarities.

- Have you both noticed the same things?
- How did the style of recording differ?
- What areas of development did you focus on?

You may find that some practitioners prefer a purely factual style, e.g. 'held bat in right hand', 'could balance on left foot', whereas others will focus on the social aspect, e.g. 'asked if he could join in the game', or physical aspect, e.g. 'could easily run the length of the garden'.

- Why do you focus on a particular aspect?
- How do you think this affects your views of child development?
- Which educational pioneer does this link with most closely?

The development of the EYFS in England

The EYFS has grown out of a range of policies, strategies and research in the early years. In 1998 the National Childcare Strategy was introduced (and updated in 2004) by the then Labour Government, to tackle child poverty, increase partnership and to break down the division between 'care' and 'education' for young children and their families (Wall 2011). The *Curriculum Guidance for the Foundation Stage* (QCA/DFEE 2000) supported practitioners working with pre-school children. There were a number of early learning goals (ELG) that set the expectations for children's achievement.

In 2002 The Education Act introduced the Foundation Stage Profile, replacing the baseline assessment. The Foundation Stage in the Act was defined as the time between the child's third birthday and the time they first receive primary education, other than nursery education (Education Act 2002, section 81).

However, there was still no guidance for the very youngest children, so *Birth to Three Matters* (DfES 2002) was developed to address this. The stated purpose was to 'provide support, information, guidance and challenge for all those with responsibility for the care and education of babies and children from birth to three years' (p. 4). In addition, nurseries and settings also had to be mindful of the *Full Day Care National Standards for Under 8s Day Care and Childminding* (DfES 2003a). This document ('the red book') detailed 14 standards and represented 'a baseline of quality below which no provider may fall' (p. 1).

Consequently, at that time, practitioners working with children from birth to 5 years old were expected to work under these three different frameworks – *Birth to Three Matters*, the *Curriculum Guidance for the Foundation Stage*, and the *Full Day Care National Standards for Day Care and Childminding*. To complicate matters even further the *Birth to Three Matters* and the Curriculum Guidance did not dovetail together, the former having four 'aspects' and the latter having six 'areas of Learning'. For practitioners looking after children from birth, this meant a whole set of new documents when the children reached 3 years old.

At around this time there were also two seminal pieces of research being completed. The first of these was the Effective Provision of Pre-School Education (EPPE) Project (Sylva et al. 1997 to 2004), the largest European 'longitudinal investigation into the effects of pre-school education and care' (Sylva et al. 2010: 1). The research investigated a range of influences on children's development, such as home learning environment, parental employment and the quality of the child's pre-school. The aims were to measure the effectiveness of the pre-school on a wide range of children from different backgrounds and to then identify which characteristics of the pre-schools made them 'effective'. For this research the criteria for effectiveness included identifying the benefits of different pre-schools and how quickly these faded over time. The research concluded that the quality was higher where settings integrated both the educational aspects and care aspects, and that the benefits of attending a quality pre-school remained evident throughout Key Stage 1 at school (Sylva et al. 2010: ii).

The second piece of research was Researching Effective Pedagogy in the Early Years (REPEY), which was commissioned by the DfES in 2002 (Siraj-Blatchford 2002) and was based on the EPPE data set (p. 9). It was developed to study, in particular, the pedagogical strategies or instructional techniques which enable learning to take place. This included the setting's learning environment as well as community and home learning environment. The research showed there were concerns about transitions (nursery to reception and reception to Year 1 in school) (p. 14) and that in those settings where there was 'continuity of learning between the setting and the home' (p. 15) the cognitive outcomes for the children were far better.

The results of both these pieces of research can be seen reflected in the EYFS. The combination of care and education comes from the EPPE, so instead of purely educational learning goals the EYFS also stipulates that a key person is statutory and that 'no child gets left behind' (DfE 2012a: 2). The continuity of care and documentation is improved by having one curriculum that goes from birth to 5 years old, which the research suggests improves cognitive outcomes. Some of the practices that were displayed in high quality settings, such as 'sustained shared thinking' (Sylva et al. 2004: vi), have also been incorporated into the Development Matters section of the EYFS, hereafter referred to as 'Development Matters' (Early Education 2012: 7).

So we can see that the EYFS was founded on the best parts of the *Birth to Three Matters, Curriculum Guidance for the Foundation Stage* and *Full Day Care National Standards for Day Care and Childminding* (DfES 2008). Since its inception in 2008 the EYFS has been reviewed (Tickell 2011) and republished with some alterations (DfE 2012b). It has retained the principles of each child being unique, positive relationships, enabling environments and that children develop at different rates – principles underpinned by the EPPE research, REPEY research and the Every Child Matters (ECM) framework. Observation is still seen as a crucial tool for informing assessment and is part of the statutory requirement (DfE 2012b: 10).

The ECM framework, which was launched in 2003 and became highly influential, is worth a mention as it brought with it a raft of changes and five outcomes for children across the range of children's services and paved the way for a more integrated way of working in early years. Its five outcomes were (DfES 2003b: 6):

- being healthy
- staying safe
- enjoying and achieving
- making a positive contribution
- economic well-being

The ECM agenda has changed many aspects of education and has been called 'arguably the most significant document to reach our desks' (Wall 2011) and 'a major piece of legislation' (Sylva et al. 2010). At its heart are universal services, working together with families and communities, to ensure that children can maximize their potential and are protected. The emphasis of having the child at the centre is clearly reflected in the EYFS, with the 'Unique Child' at the centre of effective learning (Early Education 2012).

Other curricula in the UK

This book is centred primarily on the early years curriculum in England, the EYFS. There are separate curricula for Wales, Scotland and Northern Ireland. However there are a number of similarities between all four curricula. For example, they all mention children learning through play, the importance of social development, emotional development and security, as well as a holistic environment (Scottish curriculum, p. 3), first-hand experiences (Welsh curriculum, p. 4) and opportunities through experiences (Northern Ireland curriculum, p. 6).

However there are also some notable exceptions. The Welsh curriculum 'The Foundation Phase' includes children from the age of 3 to 7 years, the Scottish curriculum 'Curriculum for Excellence' includes 3-year-olds to 18-year-olds (supported by the pre-birth to 3 guidance) and in Northern Ireland the age range is from 4 years to 6 years for the Foundation Stage, with Preschool prior to that.

Discussion box

Sometimes it is easy to get stuck with the idea that there is only one curriculum – the one you are currently working with. It can be useful to review other curricula, to find the similarities and differences, so you can make an informed judgement about the curriculum you are working with.

Choose one other curriculum from the UK (websites at the end of the chapter) and compare it to the EYFS.

- Where are they similar?
- Are there significant differences?
- Which do you prefer?
- Would you have to change your practice significantly to meet the requirements of the other curriculum?
- What does that tell you about childcare in general?

The cycle of observation, assessment and planning

In this book the focus is on the interlinking elements between observation, assessment and planning, bringing these three things together as a cycle rather than three disparate elements.

There are some excellent books on assessment, on observation and on planning. However, the missing pieces are the most important in practice. It is no good being excellent at observations if you then can't interpret them. Similarly, insightful assessments are just a paperwork exercise if they are not used in the planning process.

Therefore in this book there are explanations of different types of observations, but the majority of the book highlights how to use these to inform assessment. The aim is to answer the 'why?' question. Why have you come to that conclusion about that child from that assessment? Why have you planned that activity from that observation? This is done through links to learning theories and examples of practice.

As the practice guidance for the revised EYFS, Development Matters (Early Education 2012: 3), states 'on-going formative assessment is at the heart of effective early years practice' and should be based on observation. The cycle of observation, assessment and planning should commence at 'observation'. In addition it is suggested that summative assessment is shared with 'parents, colleagues and other settings' (p. 3).

Some definitions of terms

There can be confusion around the meanings of the various terms that are used within early years, often interchangeably. Below are some phrases with explanations of the way that they will be used in this book.

Practitioner

There has been, and no doubt will be, debate about the term used to describe the hardworking, dedicated adults who work with children. Nutbrown uses a variety of terms, including 'professional educator' (2006: xiv) and Montessori used 'directress' (1965). In this book 'practitioner' has been used to describe all those professionals working with children, including childminders, nannies and teachers. This does not prejudice against those who have good practice, but, for one reason or another, do not have qualifications.

Child initiated

A child-initiated activity is one that has come solely from a child's idea or interest. This may be from a conversation that the child has with the practitioner or from an artefact that a child has discovered. These are likely to be spontaneous activities.

Adult initiated

An adult-initiated activity is one that has been planned and conceived by the practitioner. This may be based on children's interests or observations of children, but the suggested activity has come from the adult. Is likely to be a pre-planned activity.

Adult led

Adult-led activities can be either child initiated or adult initiated. The significance is that the adult is leading the learning, through scaffolding, support or direct input into the activity. It is the adult that is leading learning and taking the activity in the direction they would like to see it go.

Child led

In a child-led activity it is the child who is directing the learning. The adult is there to observe, ensure safety and give some support. The activity goes in the direction that the child wants.

Sustained shared thinking

There is a formal definition of sustained shared thinking given by the EPPE team, which is: 'an episode in which two or more individuals "work together" in an intellectual way to solve a problem, clarify a concept, evaluate activities, extend a narrative etc. Both parties must contribute to the thinking and it must develop and extend' (Siraj-Blatchford et al. 2008).

In this book I shall be using the term sustained shared thinking in the broadest form. So this will include short conversations that give some sort of insight into the child's thinking. These may be verbal conversations, but will include ideas that are shared through doing activity together, such as building a 3D model. It is the sort of conversations and activities that go on all the time in settings, which skilled and experienced practitioners are used to having with their children.

Key learning points

The current EYFS in England has been forged from many different sources. The pioneers and educationalists have demonstrated the power of observing children at play, which has been built on by modern pioneers, such as Athey and Malaguzzi, who have put a whole new light on the complexity of children's play. Contemporary research has highlighted the difference that a 'quality' early years curriculum can make to children's lives.

Each element of the observation, assessment and planning cycle is important in its own right. However, it is essential to be able to make the elements work together in a seamless cycle to support children's learning and development.

Reflective questions

1   Can you identify any of the pioneers' philosophies in the EYFS? Consider:
   • Where does play fit into the curriculum?
   • How does this compare to Froebel and Vygotsky's theories?
2   Read the summary of the EPPE research. How has this affected the wording of the EYFS? Consider:
   • What elements of quality are now written into the EYFS?
   • What may be the shortfalls of the research?
3   Look at some other definitions of child-initiated play. Consider:
   • How do they differ?
   • Why is it important that there is common understanding of these terms in the setting?

Further reading

Graham, P. (2009) *Susan Isaacs: A Life Freeing the Minds of Children*. London: Karnac Books.

This in-depth book gives context and background material to Isaacs' life, including her role in the world of psychoanalysis and her extensive contribution to modern educational methods.

David, T., Goouch, K., Powell S. et al. (2003) *Birth to Three Matters: A Review of the Literature Compiled to Inform the Framework to Support Children in their Earliest Years.* Nottingham: DfES Publications.

This document contains some fascinating insights into the research and rationale behind *Birth to Three Matters*. This includes discussion on holistic development, continuity of learning and resilience, as well as an overview of educational theories and theorists.

Northern Ireland's curricular guidance for pre-school education http://www.ccea.org.uk/

Scottish Curriculum for Excellence http://www.educationscotland.gov.uk/earlyyears/curriculum/index.asp

Welsh Framework for Children's Learning for 3- to 7-year-olds in Wales www.wales.gov.uk

2   Why observe?

*Adults need to make detailed and sensitive observations to really 'see'
what children are doing, to make sense of their actions, to recognize
their achievements and to create further learning opportunities.*

(Nutbrown 1996: 47)

Chapter objectives

- To investigate the reasons why we observe children
- To explore some of the wider implications
- To help define a 'good' observation

Chapter overview

This chapter explores the reasons for observing children. Observing a
child at play may initially seem like the easiest thing in the world to do. I
have often had practitioners say 'but I'm not doing anything!' when I've
suggested that they stand back and just watch the children. In fact, making good observations is a skill which needs to be learned and practised.

Before making an observation, it is essential to consider the reasons
for doing it. This will determine the sort of information you record, the
method of doing it and what you will be using the information for afterwards. In this chapter some of the most important reasons for observing children are explored. In addition ethical considerations and being
respectful of the children are considered. Who are you going to share the
observations with and what is the process for this?

Finally the elements of a 'good' observation are examined: what sort of
information you should include, and which information is helpful to include.

Introduction

The observation, assessment and planning cycle most naturally starts
at observation. It is the bedrock upon which all else is built. Without

knowing your children, understanding their interests and existing knowledge, you cannot plan meaningful, challenging and exciting activities for them. It is every practitioner's *statutory* duty to 'consider the individual needs, interests, and stage of development of each child in their care, and must use this information to plan a challenging and enjoyable experience for each child in all of the areas of learning and development' (DfE 2012b: 6).

In practice this means that every practitioner must, by law, plan challenging and enjoyable experiences. This is not possible if the children are not understood as individuals. Not all boys will like cars, not all babies will like painting their hands. To be able to challenge or further a child's knowledge, the current levels need to be known. To find out the sort of activities the child does enjoy, the developmental stage a child is at, or whether they demonstrate schematic play, careful and valid observations must be made.

Although in this chapter some reasons for observing children are discussed and some of the considerations around respectful, ethical observations are detailed separately, these subjects are intertwined and should be considered complementary. Without respect for the child good observations are almost impossible. If a practitioner demands a child's time, taking them away from a game, then it is unlikely that the child will perform naturally or to their best ability.

Reasons for observing children

Five main reasons for observing children are discussed here. These cover the majority of reasons for observing children, although there may be others, such as ensuring their safety and welfare or being aware of when a baby needs a nappy change.

1 Tuning into the child

Tuning into the child means getting on their wavelength, as you would 'tune in' a radio. In practice this equates to really trying to understand their favoured activities and the things that motivate a child. This may be as simple as noticing that a baby always reaches for a shiny object, or that a toddler becomes more animated when a particular piece of music comes on. This can only be truly achieved by spending time with the child, with their social group and in different environments. For example very often children behave differently outdoors to when they are indoors.

The practitioner has to be responsive to the child's needs. Montessori (1949) identified sensitive periods when children seem to have a strong attentiveness to a particular area of development, absorbing information and learning most effectively. Curtis and O'Hagan (2003) call these 'prime times, when the brain will develop in specific areas' (p. 32). By identifying these times through observations, the child's development can be supported and learning reinforced. By 'tuning in' to the child, or fully understanding their likes, dislikes and stage of development, the practitioner can make informed decisions as to activities and resources to provide.

In practice it is sometimes easier to tune into certain children than others. For example, some practitioners have an affinity with boisterous boys where others may prefer babies. Because there is such a difference in children between the ages of 0 and 5, it is to be expected that practitioners may prefer one age range to another. This can be used to advantage, by matching practitioners and their preference, but sometimes this is not possible so practitioners should learn how to tune into the child at any developmental stage.

2 Schema spotting

As children develop, schemas may become more evident. Schemas are defined by Athey (1990) as 'patterns of behaviour and thinking in children that exist underneath the surface feature of various contents, contexts and specific experience' (p. 5). Nutbrown (2006: 10) extends this to patterns of 'action and behaviour'. Schemas then are the repeated actions of children exhibited during their play, drawings and speech.

For example, for a child with a transporting schema, carrying (transporting) objects is the most important or engaging part of their play. Typically, a 'transporter' will pack everything into bags, prams or buckets and carry it around the setting. Sand play may consist of carrying the sand to the water tray. The bikes outdoors will be used to transport toys.

There are many different identified schemas. Athey (1990: 62) describes 10 graphic, 11 space and 9 dynamic schemas, which vary from transporter to going through a boundary.

It is useful to be able to identify or spot a child who has a strong schema because the practitioner can use that knowledge to select activities that will engage the child. For example, if a practitioner wishes to engage a 'transporter' in some mathematical development, then counting toys into a pram, pushing them to the other side of the room and counting the toys out again is likely to be an engaging game. A very practical book to use for activity ideas is *Again! Again! Understanding Schemas in Young Children* by Sally Featherstone (2008), which gives lots of ideas for schematic play in each of the areas in a setting, such as water, sand, outdoors, etc.

It should be noted that not every child has strong schemas; some children may only display schematic play for a short period of time before moving onto another schema and some children may never display schematic play. Observing schemas and including this information in planning is covered in Chapter 3 and Chapter 6 respectively.

3 Special educational needs

In some cases a child may have diagnosed special educational needs (SEN) from birth. However, a lot of children are not diagnosed until later in life. A diagnosis of SEN can only be made after a significant number of observations have been completed. These may be to demonstrate a lack of progress or plateauing of development or a developmental delay in a specified area of development, such as speech and language. The significance of accurate, dated observations cannot be overemphasized in these circumstances. Without the evidence of the observations, tracking development accurately is impossible. There is further discussion about the requirements for children with SEN in Chapter 9.

4 Key person

It is currently a statutory requirement of the EYFS that every child attending a setting must have a key person. The key person will have some knowledge about their key child before they start at the setting, from the home visit or the registration information. It is usual that the key person would meet the carer on arrival at the setting, to have a chat with them and record any information about the child, such as being tired after a late night. This is particularly important for babies and children who are unable to communicate verbally with practitioners. At picking up time, the key person hands the child back to the carer, with any comments about the day. Where a key person is not present for both arrival and departure times, a second or 'deputy' key person may stand in. The key person and deputy then communicate to pass on any messages. The key person is the essential link between home, the setting and the child.

The key person will record a lot of the observations for their key child. It is usually the key person's responsibility to ensure their children's profile or records are kept up to date, using these observations.

Information box

Attachment theory

It is important to have a named, key person assigned to each child because, as we learn more about John Bowlby's attachment theory (1983), it is becoming clear how vital good attachment is for the welfare of the child.

Bowlby was first asked to look at separation issues after professionals noted the distress of Second World War evacuee and orphaned children. He started by observing young children and finding patterns of response to defined situations, such as loss of the mother figure (p. 4). This was very different to psychoanalysis of the time, which was more concerned with defining symptoms and working back towards a theory.

He found that children need to make a secure attachment to a 'mother-figure', although he later made clear that this may not be a mother, but a significant adult in the child's life, an 'attachment-figure' (p. 177). He suggested that the child needed the primary care giver to be there when needed, to be reliable and dependable. This means that the care giver had to be close physically and to be emotionally available as well.

Bowlby explored the characteristics of attachment and how attachment affected children and their development. Where children have a carer or parent who is close, available and responsive they make 'secure' attachments (p. 27). He postulated that the sensitive period is during the first year of life (p. 223) when an attachment is made to a particular figure, in preference to all others. He also suggested that between 6 and 9 months babies will start to fear 'strangers' or people who are unfamiliar to them.

Conversely, if attachments are interrupted in any way, for example the carer being in hospital for a significant period of time, then the attachment may no longer be 'secure', but may become 'avoidant' (p. 334) or 'ambivalent' (p. 337). Mary Ainsworth (Pound 2005) extended Bowlby's work, adding anxious-avoidant and anxious-ambivalent as behaviours.

Now well established, attachment theory and its implications have been extended by many other researchers (David et al. 2003; Elfer et al. 2003; Elfer and Dearnley 2007).

Practitioners can begin to understand the importance of a close, trusting and loving relationship by understanding attachment theories. If a child does not achieve a secure attachment in the first few years of life, this will affect relationships later on in life. The attachment would ideally be with a parent, but if this is not possible, then attachment with another figure will still give all the benefits. These include (Pound 2005):

- self-confidence
- efficacy
- self-esteem
- capacity to care for others and to be cared for
- mastery disposition.

Practitioners can become concerned that their attachment to a child will replace the child's love for their mother. However, a child should be able to attach to several adults with no ill effects. In Nutbrown and Page (2008), Dr Page talks movingly about her personal experiences of attachment and working with children. She suggests that this commitment and care should be termed 'professional love' (p. 184). This is inextricably linked to the concept of the key person, the importance of which 'cannot be overemphasized' (p. 186).

5 Research

Research may be a formal requirement of a degree course perhaps as a dissertation, which requires a literature review, a research methodology and so on.

However, research observations are not just for the purposes of academic study. It is more likely that a more informal type of observational research is going on every day, for example, changing the dressing up clothes to see if more children play in that corner or trying babies with their first feel of paint on their feet. The observations are taken before and after the change to see what the differences are. From this conclusions can be drawn as to whether the change is effective and therefore worth continuing. These sorts of observations happen all the time, probably without the practitioner even noticing, and are important in answering the 'I wonder what if...' questions that every reflective practitioner should be asking themselves.

Before starting

Before any observations are started, there are some considerations about the methods of working with young children. In this section the ethics of observing children and being a respectful observer are explored.

Ethics

Observing and interacting with young children is a pleasure and a privilege. Practitioners should be aware that being involved with children also means having responsibilities for their own actions and always being aware of the children's rights. This includes allowing the children not to be involved with activities: in brief, to act in a moral, ethical manner.

Informed consent

Parents must give their written consent before practitioners may start observing the child, taking photographs or making records. Most settings now have a blanket cover letter, where parents sign to give consent for their children to be photographed and observed while at the setting. Some settings include video and digital media in these as well. The use of this material should be made explicit. For example, will it appear on a website? If so, for how long and will the child's name be used? The letter should be kept up to date and a check kept that every child is included.

In general, observations can only be shared with outside agencies with written permission from the parents or carers. This includes development files being passed onto school or another setting. The exception is in cases of suspected abuse when providers must notify their child protection agency 'without delay' (DfE 2012b: 14).

A cautionary note on parental consent. It is worth checking that the person signing actually has the power to give consent. The issues around unmarried partners, blended families and newly adopted children should be investigated. On occasion the parent or carer may not have the legal power to give consent, for example if the adoption is not legally complete yet. This is termed 'Parental Responsibility' and was established in the Children Act (1989). More details about this can be found at www.gov.uk. It is good practice to include a section on the registration forms requesting who has parental consent, to save any confusion later on.

It is ethically sound to have the child's consent as well as parent's consent. Children are naturally at a disadvantage with adults, because of the 'power differential' (Cohen et al. 2007: 54). Children naturally want to please adults and know that adults are 'in charge'. So gaining consent means ensuring, as much as possible, that the child understands what is involved with the practitioner observing or photographing them. In this digital age, most children now know you can see the image at the back of the camera and ask to look at the picture. By showing children the image immediately, practitioners have an opportunity to check with the child whether they give their consent to keep it or not.

Where babies and small children are concerned the consent may be as simple as the child smiling, being content or coming over to join an activity. For older children it is appropriate to ask if it is 'OK to watch them play' or ask to join an activity. If a child refuses permission to be videoed or take part in an activity, this should be respected, however frustrating!

The United Nations Convention on the Rights of the Child (UNICEF 2012) clearly states in Article 3 that 'in all actions concerning children...the best interests of the child shall be a primary consideration'. This should be considered when doing observations. For example, is the activity set up to meet the needs of the practitioner or following the needs and interests of the child?

Being respectful of the child during observations

Being respectful to children is about listening to their views and paying attention to their wishes. As Siraj-Blatchford (1996: 24) comments, 'The way children feel about themselves is learned and every child should have the right to feel good about herself'. It should always be kept in mind that the child's interest, development and welfare are at the centre of everything that practitioners do. This is enshrined in the Children Act 1989 which, according to Curtis and O'Hagan (2003), stated that the 'welfare of the child is paramount and allowed children's opinions to be taken into account' (p. 18). They go on to discuss emotional abuse, which can be as simple as withholding praise from a child (p. 20). When observing this means always being alert to the child's welfare and ensuring this is never obstructed in any way.

Practitioners should be aware of how their own views and personal experiences may affect their observations. Being aware and making allowances for this is called reflexivity. Cohen et al. (2007) define it as how the practitioner's 'values, attitudes, perceptions, opinions, actions, feelings etc. are feeding into the situation being studied' (p. 310). It is sometimes referred to as holding a mirror to ourselves and shows a level of professionalism. For example, what is your attitude to risk? Would you allow a child to climb on a chair? Do you think only the girls should wear princess dresses? The practitioner's views could, subconsciously, affect the observations. So in the examples above, is the child climbing on the chair exploring their physical boundaries and problem solving or is that child displaying difficult behaviour? Is it 'wrong' for boys to wear dresses? If so, why?

Similarly labels and stereotypes must be avoided. In the statutory framework of the EYFS, practitioners must provide for 'equality of opportunity and anti-discriminatory practice, ensuring that every child is included and supported' (DfE 2012b: 2) and also have equal opportunities policies and procedures for children in their care (DfE 2012b: 26). Clearly this has to include language and attitudes towards observing children. For example, allowance should be made for 'cultural norms', such as girls being expected to assist boys in some cultures. This could mean that the boys are less independent.

What is a 'good' observation?

For an observation of a child to be useful and meaningful, it must have four components: the child's name, the date, the time and the observation. It is good practice to have the practitioner's name included as well.

1   *Name of child or children* The child(ren) being observed need to be identified, so the information can be used in assessment, planning and record keeping. This could be using initials, to aid the speed of writing or to protect a child's identity. On the whole the reader should be able to identify the child easily from the observation.

2   *Date* Without a date the observation becomes meaningless. The age of the child cannot be fixed and so the significance of child development cannot be deduced. If a child is counting to 100, for example, this is a beyond expectations for a 2-year-old, but reasonably normal for a 6-year-old. When tracking special educational needs it is the *rate* of progress which is significant. A slowing down, or plateauing, of development over time could be an indication of a special educational or additional need. The rate of development can only be calculated by comparing dates on observations. The date itself may be significant. For example, it could be a day when the child was unwell. If so, this should be factored into any assessments.

3   *Time* The time of day may be a very important factor of the child's behaviour and is useful to help see patterns emerging. For example, is a child always upset close to going home time, when other parents are arriving?

4   *Practitioner's name* Ideally the practitioner should sign or initial the observation, in case there are any questions afterwards. This also enables practitioners to track their own observations, to ensure that their observations cover all six areas of learning and development or include indoors and outdoors observations, for example.

These four criteria are essential for a good observation, to track a child's development and to be accountable.

Content

The content of the observation is paramount. The type of content depends on the type of observation. Different types of observations are considered in more detail in the next chapter. In general the content should be:

Factual

The exact occurrence must be recorded, preferably without any interpretation. Nutbrown (1996) describes this as 'crucial to see what is really happening and not what adults sometimes suppose to be happening' (p. 45). For example, a good observation could be 'John cried for about five minutes when dad left him at nursery'. A poor example of this same occurrence would be 'John cried because he didn't want his dad to go'. In the second case there is no indication of for how long or how upset John was, and the interpretation may subsequently be wrong – John may have been hungry or in need of a nappy change. Interpreting the actions of the child, rather than just recording the facts, may mean practitioners miss patterns of behaviour. In this example it could be that John misses his dad, but it could also be that he always comes in hungry, so needs to have a bottle prepared for when he arrives. This may not be spotted if it is always assumed that he is crying for his dad.

Accurate

It almost goes without saying that the observation should record what actually happened. This is why it is best to record incidents as they happen, rather than waiting until the end of the day and 'writing up' the day's observations. By this time other things will have happened and it would be unreasonable to expect practitioners to remember precise details of previous incidents.

Detailed

Depending on the type of observation, the level of detail will differ. However, there should be sufficient detail to make the observation meaningful. This may include time and length of time the incident occurred; other children present; exact toys being played with and possibly location (indoors, outdoors). This is particularly important when investigating schematic play. As an observation 'playing on the bikes' gives no schema information. 'Riding round in circles on the bikes, watching the wheels rotate' suggests there may be a rotational schema.

The skill in writing observations comes from knowing which facts to include and how much detail is needed. This partially comes from experience of doing observations, but also from having a clear rationale for doing the observations. So when spotting schemas, it may be pertinent to include more detail about *how* the child is playing with the toys (using to transport, envelope, rotate?) rather than just the toys being used.

Sharing observations

Sometimes observations need to be shared with other professionals. For example, it is a good idea for the key person or other practitioners to share observations with parents or carers. This can give extra context to the child's play, such as reinforcement that the child is also fascinated with the washing machine spinning and other rotational toys at home.

The parent's observations and comments can be included on the observation sheet. At Pen Green research centre in Corby, Dr Whalley has taken this even further with the 'Pen Green Loop' (Whalley 2007: 126) where parents formally observe children in their home and the observations are fed back to the nursery staff. This requires parents to be trained in observation and to attend a feedback meeting each week, so this may not be suitable for all parents. However, parents can be encouraged to give even brief feedback about their child's play at home.

Key learning points

Before an observation is made there are two considerations. First, what is the reason for this observation? Is it because I need to know more about the child and their interests? Or is it because there is an SEN worry? This will inform the details of the observation and how it is recorded.

Second, the ethics of the situation need to be examined. Do I have consent, from parents and carers, but also from the child? Am I being respectful when I watch them, talk to them and join in their games? And finally, is the content of the observation factual, accurate and sufficiently detailed to be useful?

Reflective questions

1 How often do you consider *why* you are doing an observation? Is it just part of the paperwork that has to be done? Consider:
   • the types of observations you do each week;
   • which children you observe;
   • which categories these mainly fall into;
   • whether you could do observations for other reasons.
2 What sort of guidelines do you have in place to ensure children are respected whilst being observed? Consider:
   • How do the children know they have a choice in joining an activity?
   • What are your inclusion policies?
   • Do you have an ethics policy?
3 How often do you monitor the content of observations? Consider:
   • How often do you check that observations are accurate records?

- When do you discuss and share observations with colleagues?
- What is your policy and procedure for sharing observations?
4 How are the principles of ethical, respectful observations explained to new members of staff? Consider:
  - Are there assumptions made that new staff 'know' how to observe?
  - How could you support staff?
  - How would you identify learning objectives for them?
  - Do the staff fully understand the implications of attachment?

Further reading

Nutbrown, C. (2006) *Threads of Thinking*, 3rd edn. London: Sage.
For schema spotting this is the most accessible book. It has plenty of relevant examples and a good section on books that may be used to support different schema.

Whalley, M. (2007) *Involving Parents in their Children's Learning*. London: Sage.
This is a great source of information about involving parents as well as respecting children's interests.

Peter Elfer has written extensively about emotional well being and the key person approach. Two particularly interesting pieces are:

Elfer, P. and Dearnley, K. (2007) Nurseries and emotional well being: evaluating an emotionally containing model of continuing professional development, *Early Years: Journal of International Research and Development*, 27(3): 267–79.

Elfer, P., Goldschmied, E. and Selleck, D. (2011) *Key Persons in the Early Years: Building Relationships for Quality Provision in Early Years Settings and Primary Schools*, 2nd edn. London: David Fulton.

3 Different methods of observation

Observation is a skill almost anyone can develop. It is a kind of perceptive watching, an informed way of looking that raises awareness and sharpens understanding. It helps bring to notice what might otherwise be overlooked.

(Fawcett 1996: 3)

Chapter objectives

- To explore in detail the different methods of observing children
- To critically examine the benefits and challenges of each method

Chapter overview

This chapter takes a detailed look at a wide range of observational techniques. Some of the classic techniques are suitable for everyday use, whereas others are more suitable for finding specific information, for example when the setting's environment is being assessed. Each technique has benefits and challenges for practitioners, which are discussed individually.

It is crucial that practitioners are able to use a range of observational techniques. Without being able to use this range there will be elements of children's play, interactions, environment and additional needs that may go unnoticed and unrecorded. Practitioners need to be aware of new (and easier to use) technologies, which are being introduced all the time. For example, a video camera that children can use themselves could be an informative way to record social interactions between friends, without the intrusion of an adult observing them.

Most importantly, whichever way of recording observations is chosen, the best interests of the child must be kept at the heart of the observation.

There are some really good books on observations and how these can be done well (Sharman et al. 1995; Fawcett 1996; Hutchin 1996; Riddall-Leech 2008). With that in mind this chapter discusses the observational techniques most frequently used in settings and compares them in terms of time, difficulty and situational use. In each case the role of the adult in keeping the child at the heart of the technique is considered. In general, whenever observations are recorded with the child's involvement, the child is more likely to share the experience with parents and carers. This encourages a two-way conversation with parents and setting or child-minder, strengthening the parent partnership.

The role of the child

It used to be that observations were done 'on' children rather than 'with' them, almost as scientific experiments. In one notable case, Sigmund Freud, children were not present at all – 'Freud's "model" of child development was largely derived from his reflections on his adult patients' recollections of childhood experiences and was not based upon observations of children' (David et al. 2003: 41). It is enshrined in the United Nations Convention on the Rights of the Child (UNCRC 2005) that the best interests of children must be a primary concern (Article 3), children have a right to say what they think should happen (Article 12) and they have the right to freedom of expression (Article 13). This gives children the right to say 'no' to being observed, which must be respected by the adult. Children may express their desire not to be observed in writing, drawing or by physically removing themselves. Practitioners must be sensitive to babies and young children who may express their wish not to be involved by becoming distressed or upset.

It is much better practice to work with the children, with mutual respect. Children should be considered to be partners in the observational process, whether they are actively participating or unaware of being observed by an adult. In Chapter 2 we have already discussed the ethics and respectfulness that are essential when working in partnership with young children. When using any of these observational techniques you should be respectful of the child's needs and feelings at all times. For some of the techniques, it could be that having the child as a participant in the observation would be advantageous. For example, your child may ask to put an item in the folder of work or to add their own comments to the learning story.

It is unlikely that you will be able to make written observations for long without a child coming up and asking 'What you doing?' You should be prepared for this and either have a colleague on standby to distract the child (if necessary) or be prepared to leave writing up the observation until later. It's always useful to have a spare pad of sticky back notes and pencil to give to children, so they can make 'notes' too.

Parent partnership

There is plenty of evidence to show that parents make a difference to their children's educational outcomes. The Parents, Early Years and Learning (PEAL) organization believes that 'Parents are a child's first and most enduring educators' (NCB 2007). Professor Desforges goes even further, stating 'what parents do with their children at home... is much more significant than any other factor open to educational influence' (Desforges 2003: 91). With this in mind, parent and carer comments must inform observations as well. This can be achieved by having a section at the bottom of the observation for parents and carers to fill in at their leisure, or can be completed with the practitioner acting as scribe, in the setting. Be wary of this becoming just a 'box to tick'. Parent and carer comments should be read and incorporated into the child's personalized provision and responded to as necessary.

Observational techniques

We now move on to consider a range of observational techniques. Table 3.1 summarizes these various techniques, highlighting advantages and disadvantages, and starts to make links to assessment and planning. The number of stars indicates the amount of time needed – the more stars there are, the more time is needed.

Magic moments

Brief observations can be recorded on sticky back notes or labels, which can be transferred directly into learning journeys or folders. This method of doing short observations is incredibly useful for everyday note taking. The notes are quick to use and quick to transfer into a permanent record. Very often practitioners will carry a pad with them around the setting so they can make notes of things as they happen. You will also often see children doing the same! Seeing practitioners using writing in the setting in this way can fascinate children. It is an excellent way to demonstrate writing for a purpose.

Sometimes practitioners comment that this method produces scruffy records, which they would not like to show to parents or Ofsted. However, handwritten records demonstrate the personal touch, which allow the practitioner and child's personality to shine through, which is something stock phrases cut and pasted from a document are unable to do.

Table 3.1 Observational techniques

Observation method	Time	Advantages	Disadvantages	Assessment	Planning
Magic moments	*	Easy to write up Capture fleeting moments of development	Practitioners need to be aware of child development so they can spot a magic moment	Formative assessment	Daily planning Weekly planning
Learning stories	*****	Descriptive, detailed with written and pictorial evidence	Takes time to assemble the photos, written work Key person	Longitudinal formative assessment Sharing with parents	Medium term planning
Narrative	***	Detailed Can be planned in Can be focussed on one area of development	Needs practitioner sole attention for short time Key person	Getting to know the child's interests Formative assessment	Weekly planning
Time sample	**	Better idea of child's interests throughout nursery	Need to remember to do it May need practitioners in several rooms if free flow play	Identifying and making links between child's interests Highlights areas where highest level of involvement	Daily planning
Tracking	*	Can identify which parts of the setting are being used	May need practitioners in several rooms if free flow play	Understanding a child's routine around the setting Settling in	Daily or weekly planning
Sociogram	**	Identifying friendship groups	May need full attention of the practitioner to spot fleeting conversations	Identifying and evidencing social development	Weekly planning Key group planning

Table 3.1   *(Continued)*

Observation method	Time	Advantages	Disadvantages	Assessment	Planning
Antecedent, Behaviour, Consequence and Decision	**	Rounded picture of behaviour Clear targets	Practitioner needs to witness antecedent Context needs to be understood	SEN Behavioural development Setting targets	Medium term planning
Photographs and Video	***	Record everything and can review at leisure later Children enjoy reviewing	Children may play to the camera if they know they are being recorded Some skill needed to capture right things	In-depth analysis SEN Spotting brief interactions Verbatim observations Understanding interactions	Medium term planning e.g. spotting schema
Focus child	*	Ensure that every child is observed in setting Different views from different practitioners	Child may not 'perform' that day May get several observations the same	Can pinpoint development in all areas	Personalized provision based on a range of views

Learning stories

Learning stories are, as the name suggests, the story about a child's learning and development. Podmore and Carr (1999) devised learning stories as a result of research carried out in New Zealand on assessment in their early years curriculum, *Te Whāriki*. They explain how learning stories are based on a set of five sequential behaviours or learning dispositions, which have observable criteria. These are:

- taking an interest
- being involved
- persisting with difficulty or uncertainty
- communicating with others
- taking responsibility.

For each disposition, there are three levels, which increase as mastery of the disposition is acquired: being ready, being willing and being able. For example, 'taking an interest' progresses from *expectations that people, places and things can be interesting* (being ready) to *select or construct interests in this place* (being involved) to *abilities and funds of relevant knowledge that support their interests* (being able) (Carr 2001: 24).

The stories should be positive (what the child can do) and start from something the child has chosen to do, or how a child has reacted to a provocation. There should always be photographs to accompany and illustrate the comments being made. It is important to note that the photos are to support the narrative or story, which is very different to a series of photos with captions. Hutchin (2012b) suggests that these learning journeys are completed for each child once every three months (or every term).

Drummond (2010) suggests eight things to look for when observing the child for a learning story:

1   initiative
2   engagement
3   intentionality
4   relationships with others
5   dispositions and approaches to learning
6   representation in other forms
7   sharing with others
8   reflection.

He goes on to describe the best practice when writing a learning story:

> The story must be written in the first person, as if you were a narrator talking to the child. The narrative should be from your own perspective, describing the things that the child does and says (recording dialogue verbatim as well) and paying close attention to exactly what is happening. There should be a paragraph entitled 'What it means' which describes the significance of the events. This may be written with further information from other practitioners and parents, as well as drawing on your existing knowledge of the child. If this is written so it can be read directly to the child, use the second person ('you were painting...'), just as if you were talking to the child.
>
> There should also be a paragraph entitled 'Opportunities and Possibilities', which is a description of next steps or where the observed activity could lead. Finally there should be a space for parents or carers to write their view of the learning story. They can either write them in directly or you can scribe their comments in for them. The learning story should always have a title.
>
> (Drummond 2010: 1)

As well as the mechanics of writing a learning story, it should not be forgotten that they are first and foremost a 'story' about a child, so you should be able to recognize the child, their personality and traits from the story. Hill (2009) adds that, compared to other genres, learning stories should be 'less clinical, less concerned with keeping interpretation out of the recording' as well as being 'more interesting and engaging than an anecdote and more lively and dynamic than objective field notes' (p. 2).

Learning stories are very much about keeping the child at the centre of the observations. Because they are written in the first person, just as if the practitioner is talking to the child, it makes the learning story a very personal way of recording the child's progress and significant milestones. By constructing the learning journey with the child, the child's responses and thoughts can also be recorded.

Narrative

A narrative observation is a written account of an event or series of events as they happen. The practitioner can record anything that happens at the time. This may include what the child does, says, who they play with, level of involvement, amount of enjoyment and any other contextual information. It can be detailed and may be supplemented with a photo of the activity.

The practitioner can choose to do this sort of observation at any time during the day. It is best if it is done without the child noticing so the practitioner gets a totally natural response. Ideally the practitioner should try to record a child's talk verbatim. Sometimes it can be used to record a particular area of development, such as speech and language, or sometimes it can just be a detailed view of a child's global development. It is a good habit for practitioners to do these on a regular basis particularly for their key children. It enables practitioners to keep track of general development and to identify interests, likes and dislikes. They can be done as independent, stand-alone observations or as a series of observations, for example observations of physical development over a series of months.

This is the best method for recording episodes of sustained shared thinking, recording the dialogue as accurately as possible, including errors in grammar and syntax, so progress can be demonstrated at a later date when these are corrected. The observation itself can be as long or as short as time will allow. This means that the practitioner can do it at a convenient time during the day. Ideally they should be accompanied by one or more photographs of the child, to illustrate exactly what was happening at the time.

Time sample

The time sample is when an observation is made every five minutes over a period of an hour, or several hours if possible. The observation needs to be accurate, but could be brief, maybe a comment on where the child is playing, the type of play they are engaged in or the toys they are playing with. The practitioner needs to be available to make regular observations. This can be problematic in settings where there is free-flowing play or children going into different rooms for different activities. Practitioners may sometimes share the observations, making a note if the child enters their room, or practitioners may be able to swap rooms, following the child.

This sort of observation is very useful for gauging a child's level of involvement and the types of play they're interested in. For example it may be noted that a child moves away from the activities every few minutes, except when in the construction area where they stay for 20 minutes. It can give evidence of a child's likes, such as doing a variety of creative activities throughout the morning, and dislikes, such as not visiting the writing area at all during the morning.

The disadvantage with this sort of observation is that the practitioner has to be available to keep track of the child and be able to make notes. This is not an easy task in a busy nursery environment, and observations can easily be missed. It is useful if the practitioner can use short notes to speed the process up. Conversely, it is an ideal way for childminders or nannies to keep records of the child's interactions throughout the day.

The advantage is that it gives a good overview of the child during the time of the observation. This could be particularly useful for a child who is settling in or is new to a childminder, so the practitioner can get to know them quickly. It is also an informative set of observations to share with parents and carers to let them know the sorts of things that their child has been engaged with during the day. It may also be useful for evidence for children who have suspected SEN such as attention deficit hyperactivity disorder (ADHD), where children are unlikely to spend any length of time at a single activity.

Tracking

Tracking observations requires a floor plan of the setting, including outdoors. The practitioner watches where the child goes to around the nursery, which areas they visit and for approximately how long they are there. This is then plotted on the floor plan with a note against each area as to how long they spend there in total. This can demonstrate not only the child's interests, such as spending a long time at the sand tray, but can also be used to identify the areas of the nursery that are most used by that particular child. This can be interesting if a child's behaviour has changed and evidence needs to be gathered to confirm this.

The setting environment can be evaluated by comparing several tracking observations to see which areas are most or least used during the day. For example, it could be that the younger children choose not to go to the book corner, demonstrating that it may not be appealing to them due to the arrangement or books available.

The advantage of this method is that only takes a minute for the practitioner to make a note of a particular child's movements, but the practitioner does have to be aware of what is happening in the room at all times.

Sociogram

Sociograms are rarely used but can be a very powerful tool in determining the social development of children. Observations are made of who the children play with and their social groups. The information this will give can help track a child's social development and can give an indication of personal and emotional development as well. It can be very enlightening to observe exactly how children play together and also, sometimes, very surprising. Grieshaber and MacArdle (2010) give some good examples of surprising, and sometimes upsetting, play in their book *The Trouble with Play*. In it they describe how a practitioner encourages a group of girls to include another child in their game of Cinderella. Reluctantly the group comply and the practitioner leaves them to play. However, during the review time it is revealed that the new addition to the group was assigned the task of being 'the piece of paper in front of the fireplace, collecting the cinders' (p. 28). Although the practitioner had encouraged the girls to play together, it may not have been beneficial for that child's self-esteem.

Information box

Social constructivism

Social constructivism states that a child's cognition is dependent upon their 'age, culture and life experiences' (Gray and MacBlain 2012: 70). This means that a child does not grow up in isolation but is affected by the experiences and social contacts that they have in life. Children's social development is a complex area, intertwined with personal and emotional development. As with most areas of childhood development, there are many theories of social development.

Arguably the most well known social theorist is Vygotsky, who was researching and writing in Moscow in the 1920s. His work was not published in English until 1962 (*Thought and Language*) and 1978 (*Mind in Society*). Vygotsky's theories are based in social constructivism and he developed the idea of the zone of proximal development (ZPD). The ZPD is the cognitive gap between what a child can do (zone of actual development, ZAD) and what they may be able to achieve with support from a more knowledgeable other. The more knowledgeable other, whether that is an adult, a peer or an older child, supports the child through the ZPD until the child has mastered that particular skill. Vygotsky suggests that, in this way, a child's cognitive development is shaped by their social relationships.

Other social theorists include Bronfenbrenner (1979) and Bandura (1977).

Bronfenbrenner theorized that children are influenced by a number of social layers or systems. These start at the microsystem (immediate family, peer group, nursery), the mesosystem (home, school) through to the exosystem (parents, employment) and macrosystem (demographic and culture) and finally to the chronosystem (transitions through time such as starting school, leaving school). Each system has an effect on the child's social development, but Bronfenbrenner felt that the family, community and society at large (macrosystem) had a significant influence on the child's development (Gray and Macblain 2012). However, he emphasized the importance of social interactions on a child's cognitive development and learning.

Bandura (1977) argued that children learned through imitation of behaviour they observed around them – for better or worse. His most famous experiment is with a doll called a Bobo doll. A group of children were shown a film where a woman was being aggressive with the Bobo doll and hitting it. Later on, when the children were allowed to play with a Bobo doll themselves, they were observed to hit the doll, imitating the behaviour they had witnessed in the film. Bandura theorized that the children were imitating what they had seen, aggressive behaviour, but that children would also imitate positive behaviour, such as expressive language when around articulate others (Gray and MacBlain 2012).

These theories highlight how crucial social development is to a child's overall development. Sociograms can be a very powerful observation tool in supporting and identifying this development.

Antecendent, Behaviour, Consequence and Decision (ABCD)

The observations are made of not only the incident (**B**ehaviour), but also the **A**ntecedent, that is what happened prior to the behaviour. From this the **C**onsequence is determined and the **D**ecision on how to approach any further behaviour (Riddall-Leech 2003). This can be particularly useful for SEN evidence (see Chapter 9) because it gives a rounded picture of the behaviour and may pick up 'triggers' for behaviour, such as change in routine.

This type of observation is also good for recording emotional development, particularly emotional triggers, which may not be immediately obvious. The ABCD method requires practitioners to think about the holistic development of the child, rather than one, narrow focus of development, because they need to understand the before, during and after cycle.

Photographs and video

Photographs are an incredibly strong way of recording the activities and achievements of children. Photographs very often pick up the details that it is easy for practitioners to miss in the busy environment of a setting. One photograph can show the enjoyment on a child's face, which hand the pen is being held in and who they were playing with at the time. Some of these photographs can be used in an album, which is left on a shelf for the children. They can look back and remember the activities done in the past and children they have played with. Children are often fascinated by the way they have changed over the years and they usually love remembering all the things they have done at the setting.

Video is even more powerful because it can record the speech and language of the children and capture physical movements and fleeting gazes of even the youngest children. Both video and photographs can be displayed using an electronic photo frame that will automatically scroll through the images. This may be in the setting itself or could be in a hallway where parents gather, so they can see what has been happening in the setting that day.

Focus child

In this method of observation, one or two children in the room or setting are chosen to be observed. Every practitioner and member of staff keeps observational notes on the children as they move around the setting and play in the various areas. This method gives a set of detailed observations for the children being observed. There will be observations from different practitioners, who are likely to spot different things.

The focus child technique can be particularly effective in a free-flow setting, where children are moving from room to room, indoors to outdoors. In this type of setting, it may not be possible for the key person to always observe their key child. The downside to this method is that each child may be the focus child only once every few weeks, so this method should be used in conjunction with others. This will ensure that each child will have enough observations to ensure a secure assessment. Similarly, the process of gathering all the information together from each practitioner takes time, meaning this method may not be as responsive as other methods.

Small group work

Most practitioners will have a small group of key children as part of their key person role. Very often the practitioner will have some time with their key group, away from the rest of the children. This is an ideal time to record observations of children's progress and interests. As key person, the practitioner has continuity and can see which areas of learning and development the child needs support with. It is a good time to do focussed activities that can specifically help with areas of greatest need.

Folders of work

These may be called many things, such as All About Me books, journals, personal folders, etc. They are a combination of the child's work, observations, photographs, parent and carer comments and notes from the key person. Mementos of activities can also be included, such as the tickets from a bus journey. These folders can be reviewed regularly with the child. Many children will thoroughly enjoy this and will want to look at old photos again and again.

Choosing an observational technique

The time to do different sorts of observations varies enormously, from the couple of minutes taken to note a magic moment to the many minutes taken to compile a learning story. It is important that you use a range of observational methods so you can get breadth and depth of knowledge about your children.

The methods vary in their complexity and skill required. If you are just starting to do observations, it is sensible to start with some of the simpler methods, such as narrative. Ironically, the shortest method (magic moment) requires a lot of skill: first to identify the 'moment' as 'magic' or special; then to record it quickly, accurately and in sufficient detail to be meaningful; finally being able to link it to the EYFS to make an assessment. If you need further information about a child's social circle, you could use a sociogram or tracking to get an overview on what is happening during the day. The focus child method is good for practitioners who like to collaborate as a team and share observations. It is extremely useful to have a critical friend (see Chapter 9) who can review your observations to ensure that their meaning is clear, and review your use of language, method used, etc.

Different people making observations

There are benefits and drawbacks to different people making observations of the same child. The benefits may be a more rounded view of the child's development because practitioners will always observe through the lens of their own experience. For example, if a practitioner is very creative then they will concentrate on the creative aspects of the activity, but if they are mathematical, they may notice patterns, shapes and numbers being used in the same activity. If a practitioner has training in a particular area, for example autism, then the observation may have more significance than for the practitioner who doesn't have specialist knowledge.

One of the disadvantages of different people making observations is that things may get missed. For example, if an inexperienced practitioner is not fully aware of the EYFS they may not realize that a child has achieved an early learning goal. Sometimes it is important to understand the context of what has happened; it may be the first time that child has accessed the messy play for example. If the practitioner doing the observation is not aware of this, it may not be highlighted in the observation.

Observing sustained shared thinking

Sustained shared thinking is defined as 'an episode in which two or more individuals "work together" in an intellectual way to solve a problem, clarify a concept, evaluate activities, extend a narrative etc. Both parties must contribute to the thinking and it must develop and extend' (Sylva et al. 2004). This describes the lovely conversations between adult/child or child/child, where an idea is discussed and explored.

These are the sorts of conversations that may start when a child brings a conker into the setting, for example, and starts to tell the practitioner all about it. The practitioner may respond by asking about the tree it came from or whereabouts on the journey it was found. The child could expand on this, giving interesting information about the sort of journey they had into the setting, how big the tree was and so on. The practitioner can learn a lot from these exchanges, from the sort of knowledge the child may have about trees to their knowledge about the local area that the child has travelled through.

Very often practitioners think this is only between adult and child, but there can be some very illuminating conversations between children, if you listen carefully:

Example box

Jack was ironing a small cloth in the home corner, using the ironing board and a pretend iron. His friend, Harri, came over and put a piece of plastic 'ham' on the ironing board, to be ironed. There followed an extended conversation about the flatness of ham:

'No, you don't iron ham'
'Why not? It's flat!'
'Cos this is for clothes, silly'
'But why is it flat then?'
'So it goes in a sandwich, look, like this'. Jack picks up a piece of pretend bread and lays the ham on it. 'See?'
'So how does it get flat, then?'
'Cos it's in the shop like that'
Jack carries on making the sandwich, adding tomato, lettuce and the final piece of bread on top. Harri picks up the sandwich and tries to put it into the toaster, but it is too wide to go in.
'I know!', he says, taking out the piece of ham. He puts just the ham in the toaster and pushes the button down. This time it fits.
'See, that's why it's flat!'

In this brief example the two boys have explored and extended their understanding of 'flat' when discussing a piece of play ham. Even though they are using pretend props, they demonstrate understanding about the use of the iron, how to construct a sandwich and how the ham can be put in the toaster.

How would you write up this observation? What sort of observation would you follow it with?

These are the sorts of conversations that will be occurring throughout the setting all the time. All it requires is a small amount of time and interest from both participants. The important aspect is the 'meeting of minds' where the learning occurs.

Sustained shared thinking should be recorded verbatim wherever possible. It is important to capture the exact words used and their syntax, because this demonstrates the knowledge and understanding the child has. It may be less intrusive to use a voice recorder or video recorder. You can then concentrate on the children's play, and transcribe the dialogue afterwards, although this does take a lot of time!

From this sort of observation, the practitioner can learn a great deal about how the child views the world, their attitudes, personal, social and emotional development, sense of self and others, community and much more. The child has the opportunity to learn about social interactions, turn taking, factual information and knowledge and understanding of the world.

Observations within the EYFS

The EYFS (DfE 2012b) has three prime areas and four specific areas in the Learning and Development theme. The prime areas are:

- personal, social and emotional development
- physical development
- communication and language.

The specific areas are:

- literacy
- mathematics
- understanding the world
- expressive arts and design.

Some forms of observations are best suited to evidence particular areas of learning and development. Sharman et al. (1995) caution against snap judgements, and that past experiences must also be taken into account. The following are some suggestions for the type of observation that may be most useful for each area of learning and development.

Personal, social and emotional development

The most effective observational technique for tracking social development is the sociogram because it records social interactions. The ABCD method could be used to evidence emotional triggers.

Physical development

Physical development is best observed using magic moments or narrative methods because some physical development such as moving 'confidently in a range of ways, safely negotiating space' as described in Development Matters (Early Education 2012: 24) may happen briefly.

Communication and language

Communication and language need to have close and highly detailed observations, such as narrative, learning stories, focus child and video.

This is particularly useful to evidence speaking early learning goals, namely children 'use past, present and future forms accurately when talking about events that have happened or are to happen in the future' (Early Education 2012: 21).

Literacy

Learning stories are very suited to evidencing literacy development, because samples of literacy work can be illustrated or included in the story. Emergent writing can occur in many forms, such as writing in shaving foam or 'painting' letters in water on a wall, which the learning story can capture well.

Mathematics

Mathematics can be observed in all areas of the setting, not just sitting at a table counting or identifying shapes. Indeed to support deep level learning mathematics should be found in all areas of play and development. To evidence mathematical learning it could be that the best way to show mathematical knowledge is to listen to children singing number songs or laying out a picnic, counting each plate out. For these reasons the narrative, magic moments or focus child would be good methods of observation.

Understanding the world

Understanding the world is about communities, the world around the child and modern technology. The focus child and small group work would be the most suitable methods of observation. Practitioners can see the child in all areas of the setting and start to build up a comprehensive picture of the child's understanding about the world. For example, the way a child plays in the home corner will reflect their view of 'home' or the things they talk about in small group work will show how they understand their own environment.

Expressive arts and design

This area of learning and development includes singing, dancing, drama and role-play (Early Education 2012: 9). The fleeting nature of many of these activities means that they would be best captured through video or audio recording. If the activity is a culmination of a number of areas, such as a nativity play or dance performance, a learning story could be used to tell the story.

Keeping observations up to date

It is essential that observations are kept up to date so that the assessments are meaningful (see the next chapter). This may mean that some of the more time-intensive methods, such as learning stories, may only be completed once a month, whereas magic moments are recorded every day. The Statutory Framework of the EYFS 2012 requires practitioners to observe children to assess their level of achievement, but also that 'practitioners should respond to their own day-to-day observations about children's progress, and observations that parents and carers share' (p. 10). In particular the progress check at age 2 needs 'ongoing, regular observation of children's development' (p. 11).

Inclusion of photographs

Photographs can be costly, especially if they are in full colour, and time consuming to print off. However, a picture or series of pictures can often tell a story so much more eloquently than pages of writing. One way of using photographs is to store them on a CD or DVD, which can then be included in the child's learning story or folders of work. There are now commercial programs available that will store all the information electronically or you can set up your own electronic accounts to keep children's data together.

The pictures on CDs can be displayed at the child's level in the setting. Children love watching themselves on a computer or TV screen and reliving the experiences they have had. It's also a great way to start sustained shared thinking about that particular day.

Information box

Observation complications – reactivity and reflexivity

Observation reactivity can be a problem when observing children. In the world of research, Cohen et al. (2007) describe reactivity as '[participants] may try harder in class, they may feel more anxious, they may behave much better or much worse than normal, they may behave in ways in which they think the researcher wishes or in ways for which the researcher tactically signals approval' (p. 410). In this case the 'participants' are the children and the 'researcher' is the practitioner. Therefore, reactivity describes the situations where children know they are being watched and react in a different way than they would normally, showing off or being shy, for example. As a practitioner you should be aware of this. If you suspect that a child is reacting to being watched, you should either do further observations another time or refer to previous observations to see if the behaviour is normal for that child. Merrell (2003) suggests doing observations in an inconspicuous place or not using obvious equipment, such as a clipboard.

The benefits of having different practitioners observe the same children, due to the different points of view, have already been outlined. As a practitioner, you should also be aware of your own views, prejudices, preferences and life experiences. Understanding and using this self-knowledge is called reflexivity. It is defined by Denscombe (2007) as 'the relationship between the researcher and the social world' (p. 240) and he goes on to say how our experiences affect the meaning we give to events and situations. This can be a very positive experience, as Diane Watt found during her research – 'my personal experiences could be an asset rather than a liability' (Watt 2007: 94). It is essential to recognize your own self, your own cultural beliefs, and your own assumptions – and to then understand how these may colour your observational judgements. This may be for better or for worse. For example, would you consider a child climbing onto the table a good demonstration of problem solving and physical development or would you be more aware of the safety risks this may imply?

Monitoring and auditing observations

There can be a temptation to set up a system of observations and then to assume everything is running smoothly. The fact of the matter is that practitioners may get behind with their regular observations, or less confident practitioners may not keep up to date. A room manager or setting manager must monitor observations to ensure they are of a high standard, up to date and being used to inform assessment and planning. Ideally these would be countersigned to demonstrate they have been seen. This also gives the managers an overview of the children's progress and the sort of activities being offered to the children. In the case of childminders, or where there is no room manager/setting manager, you must have a system of checking that your observations are relevant and recent.

It is the responsibility of each practitioner to check the quality of their own observations. A 'critical friend' (see Chapter 9) can support and challenge observations, to improve their quality.

Practical aspects

Once observations have been completed, there must be some consideration of how they are stored and shared. Very often this is a plastic wallet or envelope on the wall near the planning. Although this is a very quick method, the temptation is to store away the observations and never refer to them again. This obviously negates any benefits of doing the observation in the first place. There must be a system where observations are preserved but also easy to access and refer to. For example, this may be a temporary 'scrap book', where the observations are put into slip-in photo album pages or a lever arch A4 folder, with a section for each child.

Similarly, sharing information between practitioners about observations makes good sense. If a practitioner starts to see signs of schematic play, then this information should be passed onto the rest of the staff, so they can be aware of it. This may be done on a discrete notice board, on the back of a piece of laminated card with the child's name on the front. Another method is to have regular, but short, staff briefings where practitioners can share their observations and any next steps. This is particularly important for children who may have programme targets to aim for from multi-agency professionals, such as speech and language targets or physiotherapy targets. If every practitioner is watching and listening, then progress is more likely to be observed.

When observations indicate that the continuous provision could be improved, the reasons for this should be communicated to the rest of the team, so everyone knows why the provision has been altered. It also enables everyone to be mindful of whether the improvement is working. For example, the improvement could be moving the construction area next to the book corner, and displaying digger books to encourage the boys to engage with the books. If all the practitioners are aware of this, they can then spot any instances when boys look at the books.

Key learning points

There are a wide variety of observational techniques to suit different circumstances and different practitioner styles and experience. It is essential to use a range of techniques to ensure that all areas of learning and development have been observed adequately. Problems of reactivity and reflexivity must be addressed, as well as practical aspects of keeping observations up to date, relevant and stored in a suitable manner.

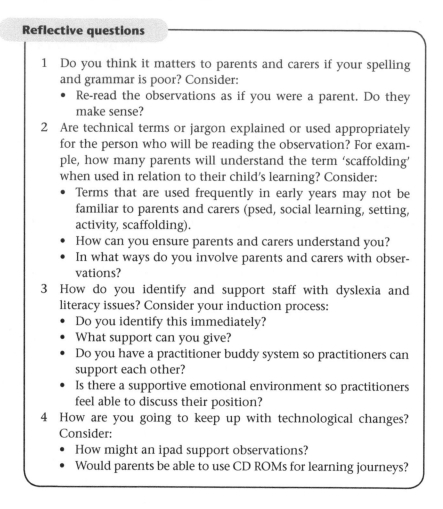

Reflective questions

1   Do you think it matters to parents and carers if your spelling and grammar is poor? Consider:
    • Re-read the observations as if you were a parent. Do they make sense?
2   Are technical terms or jargon explained or used appropriately for the person who will be reading the observation? For example, how many parents will understand the term 'scaffolding' when used in relation to their child's learning? Consider:
    • Terms that are used frequently in early years may not be familiar to parents and carers (psed, social learning, setting, activity, scaffolding).
    • How can you ensure parents and carers understand you?
    • In what ways do you involve parents and carers with observations?
3   How do you identify and support staff with dyslexia and literacy issues? Consider your induction process:
    • Do you identify this immediately?
    • What support can you give?
    • Do you have a practitioner buddy system so practitioners can support each other?
    • Is there a supportive emotional environment so practitioners feel able to discuss their position?
4   How are you going to keep up with technological changes? Consider:
    • How might an ipad support observations?
    • Would parents be able to use CD ROMs for learning journeys?

Further reading

Blaiklock, K. (2008) A critique of the use of Learning Stories to assess the learning dispositions of young children, *New Zealand Research in Early Childhood Education*, 11: 77–87.
In this paper, Blaiklock gives an interesting critique of Learning Stories. There is a full discussion of the problems of Learning Stories, including keeping the balance between observing learning dispositions and observing children's knowledge.
Carter, M. (2010) *Using 'Learning Stories' to Strengthen Teachers' Relationships with Children.*

http://www.ecetrainers.com/sites/default/files/Using%20Learning%20
Stories%20to%20Strengthen%20Teacher%20Relationships.pdf
(accessed 13 November 2012).

In this piece of literature, Carter explains how she believes Learning Stories strengthen the bond between teacher and child.

These two papers give very different accounts of Learning Stories. Compare their similarities and differences.

O'Brien, N. and Moules, T. (2007) So round the spiral again: a reflective participatory research project with children and young people, *Educational Action Research*, 15(3): 385–402.

While investigating the use of services in a local area, O'Brien and Moules found that the involvement of children was paramount to success. They draw some timely conclusions about truly listening to children rather than overlaying adults' interpretations on children's intentions.

PART TWO
Using the information

4   Assessments from observations

Without sensitive interpretation and analysis the information obtained from observing children is merely a description of what the observer has seen. To be of use it must inform our responses to children's needs, develop our understanding of children and ultimately benefit them.

(Riddall-Leech 2008: 2)

Chapter objectives

- To critically examine the definitions and purposes of assessment in the early years
- To consider best practice for assessments of young children

Chapter overview

In this chapter the reasons for assessment and its essential role in the cycle are discussed. Some practical techniques and methods are detailed so practitioners can make an informed choice. Respect and sensitivity during assessment are emphasized. But first the definitions of assessment are discussed and different forms of assessment are critically examined.

Introduction

Assessment of young children is often seen as undesirable and unnecessary, an inappropriate form of testing. However, practitioners assess children all the time. This may be informal, for example, a practitioner hearing a child counting during their play, or maybe a formal assessment for a diagnosis of an SEN, such as hearing impairment. Assessment should be considered to be a form of reflection on the observations that have been made in the setting, not as a form of testing or box ticking. Assessment should also be about understanding the potential of each child (DCSF 2010) as well as the things they can already understand, know and do. You are likely to be involved with three areas of assessment as outlined below.

Initial assessment

This is the very first assessment of a child possibly even before they start at the setting. This may be done with parents and carers on a home visit or may simply be a set of forms that a parent or carer fills out prior to the child starting in the setting. The aim of the initial assessment is to identify the child's needs so the setting may cater for those needs as well as possible. This is particularly important for babies and very young children, who cannot express their wishes. In this case it may include bottle times, nap times and methods that calm the child down, if necessary.

Initial assessment is a time to make connections and partnerships with parents and carers, as you get to know about them and they get to know about you and your setting. This is a crucial part of the assessment process as Whalley (2007) states: 'parents have a critical role to play as their child's primary educator' (p. 8).

Formative assessment

Formative assessment is the type of assessment that most practitioners will be involved in day to day and is at the heart of the EYFS (DfE 2012b). It refers to the assessment of children's abilities, interests, likes, dislikes and development and comparisons against children's typical development. From this list you can see that formative assessment is not about checklists or putting children into developmental boxes. It is about getting to know and understand the child better so that the practitioner has all the information necessary to support a child. It is about the quality of the assessment information, not the quantity. This will also include information from parents and carers at home, other settings and possibly members of the extended family.

Summative assessment

There are two summative assessments that are now required by the EYFS. One is the Foundation Stage Profile and the other is the 2-year-old Progress Check.

The 2-year-old Progress Check is a snapshot of the child's development at between two and three (Early Education 2012: 10) and is designed to 'enable earlier identification of development needs so that additional support can be put into place' (NCB 2012: 2). It should be shared with parents and carers and it is hoped that parents and carers then share this with their health visitor or health professional, so that as much information as possible about the child is known at this critical stage of development.

The Foundation Stage Profile is carried out at the end of school Reception year (when children are aged around 5) and is for use by the Year 1 teacher, as their initial assessment of the child on entering Year 1. It is a 'way of summarising each child's development and learning at the end of the EYFS' (Standards and Testing Agency 2012: 6).

Best practice and challenges

At no point in the early years should the assessments be made on a deficit model, that is to say the assessment should concentrate on what children *can* do rather than what they can't. Children's rates of development are so varied, particularly in the early years, that it is nonsense to highlight the deficits. All a practitioner can say for certain is what they have evidenced a child being *able* to do. In this respect, assessment in the early years is very different to assessment in the later education years.

It is desirable to share assessments with parents, outside agencies, other settings and between practitioners, with the appropriate, written permission of parents and carers. The important benefit of sharing information is that patterns of behaviour and insights into a child's personality may be built up from a range of formative assessments in different situations. For example, this would be particularly beneficial when identifying schema because it may evidence patterns of behaviour that are repeated elsewhere. Other benefits of sharing are that any inconsistencies may be identified, for example a child who is very chatty at home but doesn't speak in the setting. It is also very useful to give context to observations and evidence, for example a child may want to discuss a recent trip out at the weekend, but doesn't know the word 'seaside'.

Discussion box

Working in partnership with parents, carers and other settings

The value and importance of true partnership with parents cannot be underestimated. Without this part of the puzzle you can only have partial understanding of any child's learning and experience, because context is lacking.

This is supported by research. For example, it was reported in the EPPE research (Sylva et al. 2004) that in the 'excellent' settings staff shared educational aims and other child-related information with parents, and that 'parents were often involved in decision making about their child's learning' (p. 7). The report concluded that parents and carers needed to be supported as the 'first and enduring educators of their children' (p. 109), highlighting how important it is to get the parents' and carers' perspectives when assessing observations. Pugh (2010) goes even further, stating that the relationship should also be 'a more equal approach based on respect, trust, empathy and integrity' (p. 2).

From an educational point of view, one of the stated aims of the Statutory EYFS is 'partnership working between practitioners and with parents and/or carers' (p. 2) to promote 'the learning and development of all children...and to ensure they are ready for school' (p. 4). This recognizes the fact that working in partnership with parents and carers can improve the educational outcomes for children.

Sharing information with other settings is important because the settings can reinforce and extend learning, rather than repeating the same material. For example, if practitioners at one setting notice that a child is beginning to walk down the steps with more confidence, the other setting can encourage this on their climbing frame.

All assessment is a form of evaluation, which means that it is a valued and considered judgement against known criteria. In the case of early years assessment this is a judgement against a child's development in all areas, evaluated against the body of knowledge about children's learning and development. Campbell-Barr et al. (2012: 869) define this as a 'collaborative approach to making informed judgments'.

It is essential that the assessment is authentic (Grace 2001), which means that the knowledge, skill or attitude is assessed in a genuine, real life situation, not a contrived, adult-led test. For example hearing a child counting to five while laying out plates in the home corner during play, suggests that the child is competent in counting to five and understands one-to-one correspondence. Asking a solitary child to come and join an adult at a table and then count out five blocks is not authentic. The child may understand that they have to 'perform' counting, with no deep level knowledge or understanding of the numbers or their meaning. Some children may become anxious because they know something is expected of them, but may not be secure enough to share their counting skills yet. Or the child may simply not understand the premise of the exercise.

Children do not develop their skills and knowledge in neat areas or boxes. They develop holistically and randomly, sometimes displaying insights far beyond their years and sometimes unable to remember what you've just asked them. In addition, this will vary from child to child, with each child being unique in every aspect. Young children learn in a very different way to adults or even older children (Guddemi and Chase 2004), which cannot, and should not, be assessed by written 'exams' or formal tests. Young children need to express themselves with the whole of their being, during play and without any constraints. Taking all this into account, the approach to development should also be holistic to 'reflect accurately the nature of children's development and acknowledge the interrelationship between different aspects of learning' (DfES 2007: 13).

Categorizing children's learning is fraught with difficulties. Each curriculum designates different skills to different groups with different names. Guddemi and Chase (2004) suggest that children's development can be categorized into four areas – physical, cognitive, social and emotional – but also caution that each child is unique, as is their rate of development. As highlighted in the previous chapter the EYFS (DfE 2012b) subdivides learning and development into seven areas, each of which has its own early learning goals (ELGs):

1   personal, social and emotional development
2   physical development
3   communication and language
4   literacy
5   mathematics
6   understanding the world
7   expressive arts and design.

Not everyone agrees that these are suitable areas for learning and development, or even that learning and development *can* be subdivided in this way. Campbell-Barr et al. (2012) suggest that some skills seem to be more favoured than others in the EYFS and that it 'fails to acknowledge the holistic and dynamic nature of the child' (p. 865).

The assessments against the ELGs in the EYFS (Early Education 2012a) rely heavily on children being able to express themselves verbally to describe their knowledge. Just a few examples are:

- children will talk about their ideas (personal, social and emotional development, p. 11);
- talk about ways to keep healthy and safe (physical development, p. 27);
- children talk about past and present events (understanding the world, p. 38).

This presents an extra layer of problems when you have a child who has English as an additional language (EAL) or who has speech and language problems. Part of the practitioner's skill is to determine whether a child who is falling short of the ELGs is due to English not being the home language or whether is it a more serious language delay. The EYFS (DfE 2012b) suggests that practitioners should first assess a child's grasp of the English language and if they feel that it is not sufficient, then 'practitioners must explore the child's skills in the home language with parents and/or carers, to establish whether there is cause for concern about language delay' (p. 6).

One of the criticisms of having an early years curriculum is that the ELGs are setting children up to fail. This is in part due to the way they have been written. Brooker et al. (2010) maintain that those practitioners who assess children 'have many specific criticisms' (p. 36) about how the ELGs have been formulated, with some being too stringent and some not acknowledging children's further achievement (bilingualism). Some aspects of the ELGs, particularly problem solving, reasoning and numeracy, 'were criticised for their inconsistency and illogicality' (p. 44). There has also been criticism of the 'cumbersome assessment criteria' (Roberts 2011: 13) and the way that it has sometimes filtered down from the appropriate level at Reception Year to being used inappropriately in pre-schools and toddler rooms, when children are clearly too young to be assessed in this way. Campbell-Barr et al. (2012) believe that 'the EYFS profile only provides a skeleton image of the child as a learner' (p. 866).

Practitioners can also be concerned about assessing children in this way because they fear children being 'labelled' or stereotyped. For example Tannenbaum (1938) believes that 'labels' in criminology not only persist if reinforced, but also that the people would start to believe them themselves – a self-fulfilling prophecy. This usually has a negative connotation or stigma, such as boys not being interested in writing – when, in fact, they are honing gross motor skills and coordination, essential for writing ability. When this is investigated further, it is rarely the assessment that labels the child; it is more often how the practitioners use (or misuse) the assessment subsequently that has the greatest impact.

However, despite the concerns outlined, it is important that there are levels against which children can be assessed. Without these it would be much more difficult for practitioners to ensure children are making the progress expected. Just as importantly practitioners can use the assessments to identify children who may have SEN or who may be gifted and talented.

As with observations, it is again essential that practitioners are aware of their own cultural biases. For example, some cultures will expect the girls to help their brothers to dress or help to feed them. Practitioners should not see this as a negative – it is simply what the children have been brought up with. This should be dealt with sensitively and children should be encouraged to be independent.

Similarly, there should be reflection on the environment before assessments are made. For example, does the home corner mirror the child's home environment? You may see very different play if the environment is alien to the child.

Example box

Julia was playing in the home corner and invited her key person, Jan, to come and join her for tea. Jan happily accepted and sat in the corner while Julia busied round getting out plates and forks.

Jan asked 'Are you getting the saucepan?'
Julia didn't reply, but gave her a quizzical look.
Jan tried again. 'Are you going to make me some food in the saucepan?'
Julia obviously didn't understand the question.
It became clear that there was a difference of expectations, as Julia placed the play food in the toy microwave and said 'Ding!'

It may be that Julia had never seen anyone cook using a saucepan, but that all of her meals came from the microwave.

Childcare is becoming more and more commercialized, which is beginning to affect the way that parents view their childcare provision (Kitano 2011; Morton 2012). There may be unrealistic expectations about the children's development from parents, which can put pressure on practitioners to assess children's development beyond their actual development.

Record keeping

It is essential that the records kept for assessments are a 'living' document, not just something that is completed prior to a setting move or parent's evening. This is partly because it forms the basis of planning (discussed in the next chapter) and partly because children are constantly growing and learning. Guddemin and Case (2004) note how children have periods of 'rapid growth and frequent rest' (p. 3) and this should be reflected in the on-going assessments in the setting.

The links to the EYFS, Development Matters, should be clearly made, whether this is the age band, early learning goal or descriptive text. This is so other practitioners, parents and carers can clearly see the reason for the observation and how the assessment has been formed. It is also useful to demonstrate the reasoning behind assessments to Ofsted or other inspection bodies.

Links with observational techniques

The most common assessment is a judgement based on what is already known about the child from previous observations, whether what has been observed is usual or extraordinary. This is compared to the practitioner's own knowledge of child development. For inexperienced or new practitioners this may only be basic knowledge, but well qualified, experienced practitioners will be able to compare the observations with a variety of learning theories, philosophies and research interpretations. Then the judgement may be compared to the suggested development levels and ages in Development Matters (Early Education 2012). For an experienced practitioner this process may only take a minute, as something is observed, noted as being significant and mentally logged against the levels suggested in the EYFS. For practitioners just starting out, assembling and assessing all this information so quickly can seem like a piece of magic!

In the previous chapter we considered the major observational techniques available and now we explore how these methods gain value once they can be used to assess a child's achievements.

Magic moments

These are the most often used of all the observation methods but are often the least well evaluated. If a magic moment is included in a child's folder, it should be evaluated in some way. It is not enough just to include the observation and hope the reason for its inclusion is obvious to the reader. There should be a clearly stated evaluation as well. Some examples may help here:

Direct link to Development Matters (Early Education 2012) age and 'Unique Child' column, along with a brief evaluative judgement. For example:

- Observation: Thomas played in the sand for the first time today. He was smiling and let the sand run through his fingers.
- Evaluation: PSED. 8–12 months. Interacts with others and explores new situations when supported by familiar person. Thomas enjoyed exploring the sand; he seemed to like the feel on his hands.

Direct links to other programmes, such as Every Child a Talker (ECaT) (DCSF 2008a) or Letters and Sounds (DCSF 2008b). For example:

- Observation: James said 'I can hear an airplane! Its over there, near the tree'.
- Evaluation: Letters and Sounds Phase 1: Describe environmental sounds. James is good at distinguishing between sounds and can work out where a sound is coming from very quickly.

Link to a theory or philosophy:

- Observation: Harri spent 5 minutes watching the clothes in the washing machine go round. He often spins the bike wheels round as well.
- Evaluation: Possible rotational schema. Harri may have a rotational schema, which he is exploring in his play.

It may not be necessary to evaluate every sticky note that is written individually – several may build up to form a picture of development. For example, a child may play with the dressing up clothes and then return to them after lunch, but enacting a more complex story. This progression may be shown from the observations on a few sticky notes, with a single evaluation on the progression.

Learning stories

Podmore and Carr claim that 'the Learning Story framework for assessment describes the contribution that early childhood experience makes to life-long learning' (1999: 1). This is in great part due to the learning story framework having a section or paragraph entitled 'What it means', which is the evaluation of the story. Because learning stories may describe only a very short incident or activity, the evaluation may be very specific. Other learning stories may describe activities that cover several areas of learning and development, with evaluations in all those areas.

Example: The learning story may describe how Jack first rode his tricycle. The evaluation may include comments on his gross motor ability, balance, perseverance, self-confidence and ability to share. This is intended to be a reflective piece, so may also draw on previous knowledge about the child, and may include comments from parents and carers.

Narrative

The evaluation or assessment of a narrative observation will include more than one area of development. This is because of the length of the observation and the amount of detail that can be included. The evaluation may link to Development Matters (Early Education 2012), Letters and Sounds, etc. – the same as the magic moments – but there may be several links in several areas. The assessments of narrative observations should give a broader picture of the child's overall interests and motivations.

Example: The narrative observation is of Molly having her lunch in the high chair. Molly is trying to use her spoon to eat her yoghurt.

Evaluation: Molly's gross and fine motor skills are developing. She has much better control of her spoon than last week. She is exceeding her age in the EYFS, Development Matters (8–20 months) and enjoys her independence.

Time sample

Time samples are an observation of how a child uses the environment, plays with friends and accesses activities. Evaluations can be made about the child's personal, social and emotional development, for example the number of friends they play with regularly, dispositions to learning, attachment and levels of involvement. The links between the activities that the child enjoys may become clearer. For example, a child who is first mixing sand with water, then making powder paint with water, then making mud pies outside, may be exploring mixing or a transforming schema.

This is one of the observational methods that can highlight where a child's highest level of involvement is.

Example: If Jade spends 20 minutes of the hour's observation with the malleable materials, it could demonstrate a deep interest in creating 3D models or using her hands to do practical things.

An assessment for this sort of observation may be of the environment, for example, the construction area was well used, with Olivia able to get the resources easily and able to bring other materials in as well. Or the assessment may be of the child. For example, Rebecca has shown great interest in the treasure baskets this morning, playing for over 10 minutes with the keys. After that she was playing with the shiny tin. She showed obvious pleasure (giggling) at her own reflection.

Use caution when using this method to demonstrate a child's in-depth or embedded skills and knowledge: because the times are only very short, you are unlikely to have enough observation to truly evaluate this.

Tracking

Evaluation of tracking can demonstrate the child's routine around the setting and the type of activity that the child enjoys. It could be that some children always start with the same toy or area and then move to another area in a regular pattern. Other children may go to a particular practitioner and join their activity. Assessments from these observations help explain the way that children access the resources in the setting and may highlight aspects of the environment that need addressing.

Example: When evaluating the tracking it is found that David is only outside for a few minutes and then comes indoors again. He repeats this all morning. When the practitioner sits with David and asks him why, it is because the diggers and cars are indoors (David's favourite toys) and he is ferrying them outside for his play.

Tracking is also good for evaluating the areas that children are choosing not to access. For example, none of the children had accessed the book corner all morning. On assessing this, it was found that the comfy cushions had been taken for washing and not replaced, so this area was now less appealing to the children.

For children who are settling in, tracking is a good way to assess their initial confidence and social skills. For example, do they access all the areas in the setting, exploring and investigating, confident to talk to other children, or do they just stay near their key person?

Sociogram

Sociograms are good at identifying and evidencing social development. The observations may include who the children play with and for how long. The assessment or evaluation gives more details.

Example: Jody and Jade were playing outside together.

Evaluation: Jody and Jade were good at sharing their toys and were excellent at cooperating, building the dolls house. Jody was more independent than Jade, fetching more dolls, but Jade was more skilful at negotiating changes in the plan.

Antecedent, Behaviour, Consequence and Decision

The ABCD observational method is generally used when there is some concern over the child's development, whether this is behavioural or SEN. The evaluation of this method may need several observations, so patterns of behaviour may be spotted. The ABCD observational method can be used to evaluate behavioural strategies, so the observations are made before and after the implementation of a new strategy and the two sets of observations help assess how successful the strategy has been.

For older children, this is also a useful set of observations to share and talk through together, so a joint evaluation of the situation can be made.

Example: ABCD observations on Danny demonstrated that he was more aggressive on the days when Jake was at the childminder's with him. When the childminder sat and talked to Danny about this, he said that it made

Jake laugh when he 'messed around'. Danny agreed with the childminder that this wasn't acceptable and that they would work on this together.

Video

Video recording can capture behaviours, language, body language, social interactions and a whole range of children's development that would get missed in the busyness of a day. This can then be evaluated at leisure later on in the day. Practitioners may wish to look for a particular piece of evidence, for example language interactions, or an overview of social interaction for a small group. Comparing videos taken at different times can show evidence of a child's developmental progress. Sometimes the most interesting part of the video is the 'off camera' action that has gone unnoticed by the practitioner, when children think they are not being watched!

Focus child

Making observations on a focus child, using several practitioners, can give an excellent all round assessment of the child's development.

Example:
- Ann observed Thomas (10 months) playing with the books, sometimes putting them to his mouth, but then putting the book down again.
- Becky observed Thomas at lunchtime, intently watching the practitioner getting the food out and squealing when it was his turn.
- Carol observed Thomas looking round when someone said his name.

From these observations a number of evaluations or assessments can be made:

From Development Matters (Early Education 2012) Thomas is developing in a number of areas, within the expected bands for a 10-month-old baby:

- *Physical development*: explores objects with mouth, often picking up an object and holding it to the mouth.
- *Personal, social and emotional*: learns that own voice and actions have effects on others.
- *Communication and language*: stops and looks when hears own name.

Different practitioners have observed different aspects of Thomas's behaviour, so several areas can be evaluated.

Information box

Assessment for learning

Assessment for learning is defined by the Assessment Reform Group as 'the process of seeking and interpreting evidence for use by learners and their teachers to decide where the learners are in their learning, where they need to go and how best to get there' (2002: 2). It was based on research in classrooms, with older children, but still has some sound advice for practitioners working with children in the early years. For example:

Assessment for learning:
* is part of effective planning;
* focusses on how children learn;
* is sensitive and constructive;
* fosters motivation;
* helps learners know how to improve;
* develops the capacity for self-assessment;
* recognizes all educational achievement.

Black et al. further define assessment for learning simply as promoting 'students' learning' (2003: 2), instead of passing exams or populating league tables. Viewing assessment in this light could be very beneficial for practitioners in the early years. This is particularly so for those practitioners who have to complete the EYFS Profile; where there may be 'top-down' pressure to concentrate on maximizing the scale points rather than documenting the learning that has taken place over the course of the Foundation Stage.

Further reading about the original vision for schools can be found at:

Knight, J. (2008) *The Assessment for Learning Strategy*. Nottingham: DCSF Publications.

In her paper, 'Getting to the heart of authentic Assessment for Learning' (2011) Sue Swaffield discusses the difficulties of implementing and maintaining a genuine environment of 'assessment for learning'. It is an in-depth critique of how good intentions can get sidelined and has many parallels in the early years sector.

Early Years Foundation Stage Profile

The EYFS Profile is completed during the academic year that children reach the age of 5. It is a method of assessing a child's level of attainment at that point in time and can be used by the teacher in Year 1 (i.e. when the child is aged 6) to plan a curriculum to meet the child's needs. The statutory requirements for the EYFS demand that the Profile 'must be completed for all children, including those with special educational needs or disabilities' (DfE 2012a: 12). It is a snapshot of that child at the time of completion, and cannot demonstrate progress because it is a single assessment.

The Profile itself is a range of 'scale points', from 1 (at the lowest end) to 9 (at the highest end). Each area of learning and development has its own column, subdivided to match the Development Matters subheadings. These are the 'early learning goals' (DfE 2012b: 7), which match the early learning goals in the Development Matters document. The practitioner must decide whether a child has reached the level described in the scale point, or whether the child is exceeding the level or not yet reaching it (termed 'emerging'). It is a statutory requirement for the Profile to be shared with the parents and carers.

The results of the EYFS Profile are carefully moderated and monitored by the Government, via the local authorities, to ensure the reliability of the resulting data.

Information box

Reliability and validity of assessment

Reliability and validity are essential components of the observation, assessment and planning cycle, without which each element will not flow smoothly onto the next.

Vogt and Johnson (2011) define reliability as 'the consistency or stability of a measure or test or observation' (p. 336). In terms of a measuring instrument this means that it gives the same answer when repeatedly measuring the same thing. When discussing research methods, Cohen et al. (2007) explain that the meaning of reliability depends on whether the research is quantitative or qualitative. In quantitative research it means 'dependability, consistency' (p. 146). In qualitative research they state that reliability means 'fidelity to real life, comprehensiveness, detail' (p. 149).

Vogt and Johnson (2011) define validity as 'the truth value' (p. 415) of the area under discussion. This could be the trustworthiness of the statements or the accuracy of the interpretations from the information available or the appropriateness of the data gathered. Cohen et al. (2007) suggest that validity also includes the 'honesty, depth, richness and scope of the data' (p. 133).

You can see from these definitions that good observations and assessments should be: consistent, dependable, true to life, truthful (both in statement and accuracy of interpretation for assessment), appropriate, honest, in-depth and rich in useful information.

Key learning points

It is emphasized that assessment should not be about 'testing' young children, but used as a method for gathering accurate information on progress and to inform next steps. Each child is unique and develops holistically, so it is very difficult to categorize their learning and development into precise, neat areas. A wide range of assessments can, and should, be made from the different observational techniques. Assessments are an effective method for evaluating observations.

Reflective questions

1   Are you aware of your children's culture and background when doing assessments? Consider:
   • How do you gather information about your children's background and cultural influences, for example extended family?
   • How do you adjust your evaluations to reflect cultural differences?
2   Are the reasons for including magic moments clear? Consider:
   • How would a new practitioner or visitor understand the assessment?
   • Could all the practitioners explain the reasons to an Ofsted inspector?
3   Look at your observational methods. Consider:
   • Could you use a wider variety of assessment methods?
   • Why do you use the ones that you do?
   • How do you track the different methods that you use?
   • Do you use practitioners' strengths when doing observations, for example, those practitioners who have greatest knowledge of social learning theory for sociograms?

Further reading

Wexler Sherman, C., Gardner, H. and Feldman, D. (1988) A pluralistic view of early assessment: the project spectrum approach, *Theory Into Practice*, 27(1): 77–83.

This paper advocates 'assessing the child in context', meaning that children's talents cannot be assessed in isolation to their family, culture and experiences. Unsurprisingly, with Howard Gardner as one of the authors, the notion of 'intelligence' is also challenged. Although this paper was written a number of years ago there is still plenty of resonance, including school readiness.

Schiller, W. (1999) Adult/child interaction: how patterns and perceptions can influence planning, *Early Child Development and Care*, 159: 75–92. This paper focuses on motor development and how a multi-faceted approach to assessment, including teachers, parents and children, can support the child's motor development. The paper details the assessment methods and draws some interesting conclusions.

5   Deciding the next steps from assessments and observations

The important role played by observation and assessment in the Early Years in improving practice constantly and in monitoring children's progress cannot be overestimated.

(Palaiologou 2010: 13)

Chapter objective

- To explore the ways that next steps can be determined from assessments and observations

Chapter overview

This chapter deals with the vital area of deciding the next steps from the observations and assessments already undertaken. This tends to be a very poorly documented area in the observation, assessment and planning cycle but it is the critical element that makes observations meaningful. This chapter explores the different methods and strategies for deciding appropriate next steps from assessments and evaluations.

The next steps are the follow-on activities or experiences that the practitioner feels would most benefit the child. These should always be based on accurate and clear observations and assessments. As seen previously, this requires sound knowledge of child development and knowledge of the individual child's interests. All too often, next steps appear to be chosen at random, with little reference to child development or even the observations. When there is reference to child development, there is rarely any reference to the reasons *why* this would be a valuable next step for this particular child from the assessment of the observation. It is essential that practitioners understand why, as well as how, they are choosing next steps. If there is no underpinning knowledge, next steps will be vague, random and not linked in to the overview of that child's development or progress.

Categories for next steps

Next steps can fall into one of four categories:

- child development
- extending an interest
- embedding a learning point
- personal, social and emotional development

Each is considered in turn below.

Category 1: Child development

This is probably the easiest form of next step because it is so well supported by the EYFS, Development Matters framework and other development programmes, such as Letters and Sounds (DCSF 2008b). The practitioner needs to determine from the observations and assessments whereabouts the child is currently in their development. This can then be referred to in Development Matters (Early Education 2012) or Letters and Sounds, etc. as appropriate. The next step is simply the next stage of development as listed in those documents. However a word of caution is appropriate here. Sometimes the developmental next steps may be too much, or too little, for your child. This may be because your child has SEN, is gifted and talented or the developmental stages have not been evenly spread in the documents you are using. Use the suggested next step as initial guidance and then use your own knowledge of child development and the assessment of the child to create a more appropriate and finely tuned next step.

Example box

Your 8-month-old baby is confidently turning towards the sound of your voice.

In Development Matters: *Communication and language, listening and attention: turns toward a familiar sound then locates range of sounds with accuracy. Birth–11 months*
Next steps: Refer to the Development Matters (Early Education 2012) document and look for the developmental stage that follows this milestone. In this case, the next section of Development matters, 8–20 months, suggests that babies should: *Move whole bodies to sounds they enjoy, such as music or a regular beat.*

(Early Education 2012: 15)

Category 2: Extending an interest

This is a good form of next step for when you have a child who has a particularly strong interest or fascination. For example, it could be an interest in fire engines or construction or a schema. The interest may be extended by providing activities that encourage the child to access different areas of the curriculum via their interest.

Example box

Hassan enjoys playing with fire engines, but spends most of his day in the small world area, with the same toys. His key person would like to encourage him to enjoy other areas of the curriculum in the setting.

Next steps: Fire engines could be added to the outdoor play, in the paint tray or firemen hoses could be added to the water tray. Part of the music session could include sirens and noises made by vehicles, such as reversing 'beeps'. By following the child's interest in this way, the practitioner is encouraging him to access all areas of the curriculum.

Category 3: Embedding a learning point

This next step aims to embed learning that may just be emerging. For example, your child may be investigating conservation of number using coins. Adding activities can extend this, such as including objects like teddies or cars. Or you may want to take the learning in a different direction, such as conservation of mass.

This form of next step may seem very small, but don't be afraid to have activities which reinforce learning. If children are moved on too quickly, especially in mathematical development, the learning does not become embedded. Williams, in his review of mathematics teaching, identifies 'consolidating and refining skills and understanding' as being crucial (Williams 2008: 34).

Example box

Vashti is putting cups on the table, counting them out as she does so. Then she stacks them all together and counts the stacked cups, touching each, one at a time.

'Still five cups!' she says, happily.

Her key person says 'How many cups will there be if you give one to each teddy?'

Vashti thinks about this for a minute, then says, 'There will be five cups'.

Next steps: This could be extended by encouraging Vashti to count out plates and then check the number when stacked up, or counting the number of bikes outside when being used and then when they are parked up by the fence.

Category 4: Personal, social and emotional development

It has been shown that children who are secure and have a mastery disposition have a good base from which to learn (Katz and Chard 2000). By providing opportunities for children to develop their personal, social and emotional skills, the practitioner is enabling many other sorts of learning to take place as well. This form of next step, more than any other, is suitable for whole group work as well as individuals. This could also be group work across the age ranges, where different aged children can learn from each other.

Example box

Sorrel, aged 5, is playing with Ellie, 3, at the craft table. Strips of paper have been put into a cup on a shelf to one side.

Ellie struggles to reach to the top of the cup to get the strips out, so Sorrel reaches over and gets the cup down from the shelf for her, saying 'Did you want this, Ellie? Is that better?' Ellie nods happily and carries on with her picture, while Sorrel returns to his picture.

Next steps: Sorrel has demonstrated understanding and care for others. Giving Sorrel small responsibilities for looking after the younger children could extend this and provide a next step for his development. For example, Sorrel could help younger children zip up their coats or sit next to children who are less able at pouring drinks at lunchtime to help them.

In general with all next steps, do consider 'more of the same'. Children respond well to repetition and enjoy the security of knowing what is happening next. A skilled practitioner should be able to see whether the child is ready to move on. For example, children often enjoy hearing the same storybook again and again, and may not respond as enthusiastically as you had hoped when a new book replaces their favourite!

It is important for practitioners to remember that children's learning is not a linear set of achievements and that they learn across all areas simultaneously and at different rates. The EYFS recognizes this with its use of prime and specific areas. Because of this practitioners should not just try to rush children onto the next level. Creative and innovative thinking should be used to see the links between different areas of learning development and how these can support each other.

Practitioners need to acknowledge that occasionally children will take a step backwards, particularly after the long summer holidays or an illness. But there is also a value to children going back and revisiting a much simpler activity, particularly if it builds up their mastery disposition. After all, as adults we sometimes enjoy reading trashy magazines rather than textbooks!

From assessments to next steps

Using the assessment to determine next steps can be where practitioners can feel most unsure. Here are some examples of an observation and assessment, demonstrating how next steps may be chosen.

Example 1

Observation

Nathan stamping his feet and watching the light in his shoes flash: 'Look, the lights come on when I do this'.

Assessment

Nathan is exploring cause and effect. He has realized his actions cause the lights in his shoes to flash. He has calculated how hard to stamp his feet to set the lights off.

Next steps

Category 1 – child development:
Development Matters (Early Education 2012) 30–50 months, understanding the world, technology: 'Shows skill in making toys work by pressing parts or lifting flaps to achieve effects such as sound, movements or new images.'

The practitioner can 'Support and extend the skills children develop as they become familiar with simple equipment, such as twisting or turning a knob' (p. 42). The next step may be looking at other simple equipment in the setting, such as the different types of door handles or opening the fridge door to see the light come on.

Category 2 – extend an interest:
Nathan's interest may be the lights or the fact that it is flashing. This knowledge will come from knowing Nathan and understanding his interests. The next step to extend in this instance might be a fascination with light and dark, for example, using the pop-up tent and taking him in with a flashlight to see the difference in dark and light.

Category 3 – embed a learning point:
This could be more cause and effect activities. For example, if you push the button on the CD player music comes on and off. What other kinds of buttons can you find in the setting?

Category 4 – personal, social and emotional development
Enjoyment of own achievements. The next step may be to support his mastery disposition, showing his friends his flashing shoes at circle time to support his self-esteem at being able to do this. This may be appropriate if Nathan is generally shy or hesitant to speak at circle time.

Example 2

Observation

Oliver (40 months) was playing in the garden. He discovered that when he digs in the soil he can find worms and other minibeasts. He was fascinated with the way that the worms move and spent most of the afternoon looking for, then carefully watching, worms.

Assessment

Oliver is showing care for minibeasts and a very inquisitive nature. He understands that he needs to dig in the soil to find the worms.

Next steps

Category 1 – child development:
Development matters (Early Education 2012) 40–60 months, understanding the world, 'They make observations of animals'.

Practitioners can support this by 'Helping children to find out about the environment' (p. 40). This next step could be to see if Oliver can spot any worms anywhere else and dig in different parts of the garden to see where has the most worms.

Category 2 – extend an interest:
Oliver has a fascination with the way the worms move and where they live. This could be extended to other minibeasts, such as watching spiders

scuttling around in the shed or how woodlice, beetles and centipedes move and live.

Category 3 – embed a learning point:
Books on worms and a wormery in the setting would give Oliver more opportunities to find out about worms.

Category 4 – personal, social and emotional development:
Oliver has shown great sensitivity towards a helpless creature. Practitioners can support this by encouraging this caring nature and discussing emotions and feelings with him. This could be extended into social development by encouraging Oliver to share his discoveries with other children.

How to decide what to choose

Choosing next steps should not be a random action, they should be thoughtful and considered, and the reasons why the next steps are suitable should be clear to the practitioner and preferably recorded somewhere. The choice of next step must be part of a bigger picture to support the child's holistic development.

Example box

Kieran has been exploring role-play, small world play and construction for over a week. While reviewing her observations, his key person has noticed that she hasn't any observations of Kieran playing socially and is concerned about this. She makes a note to do a game-playing activity at a small group time, with all of her key children. The aim of this will be to observe Kieran's social interactions.

Sometimes there is an unintentional bias by the practitioner. We have already seen how practitioners view children's development through the lens of their own experience and knowledge, and they may also avoid, or favour, some next steps for the same reason. One particular area of learning and development that is often avoided is mathematical development. This may be because practitioners are less secure in their own mathematical knowledge or because mathematical links are not as obvious as some of the other areas of learning and development. Practitioners should review their observations and assessments to ensure that all areas of the EYFS, including the characteristics of effective learning, as described in the Development Matters (Early Education 2012) document, have been covered. A critical friend could help by reviewing your next steps on a regular basis to ensure that appropriate weighting has been given to all areas of learning and development.

Similarly it should not be forgotten that the next step may not be a specific activity but could be access to part of the environment or continuous provision, such as open-ended resources for role-play, or targeted encouragement and support by a practitioner in a particular area.

Some things to consider

As has been demonstrated the key to this part of the cycle is dependent on the practitioner having understanding in several areas:

Knowledge of the child

The practitioner needs to know and understand the child, tuning into their interests. The practitioner must be able to interpret exactly what it is that has sparked the child's interest, for example is the interest in the water play about pouring and filling, making bubbles or floating and sinking? Without this knowledge the next step activities may not be appealing or appropriate. Practitioners also need to be responsive to the child's mood or attitude at that particular time. A game requiring good concentration is not suitable for a child who is ready for a nap.

The setting

The next steps have to be practical. It is no good suggesting a baking activity if there are no baking facilities. Some settings allow food play while others don't. Alternatively, a Forest School will have plenty of opportunities to explore nature, weather and climbing, which may not be possible at other settings. At a packaway setting or a childminder's, it may not be possible to leave a large construction model overnight. These limitations may restrict some of the next steps.

Resources available

The practitioner must have some idea of the type and amount of resources available. This does not mean having to buy lots of new toys, but is about forward planning and making use of a variety of materials, including free and found. For example, planning to do fruit tasting if there are only apples available is going to be much less fun than if a variety of fruit and vegetables has already been sourced. Knowing where you can source large cardboard boxes at short notice is always useful.

Possible lines of development

Possible lines of development (PLOD) as described by Bartholomew and Bruce (1993) and popularized by Whalley and the team at Pen Green (Whalley 2007), is a method of recording next steps for children with schematic play. It is a condensed version of all the learning opportunities and experiences that you may wish to provide for a child in your setting. Whalley (2007) uses them to support schematic play and also for ideas to support groups of children with similar schema.

The child's, or children's, names are placed at the centre of a circle. The seven areas of learning and development radiate from the centre. Activity ideas are put alongside each area of learning and development. These provide a platform from which other ideas can be launched and incorporated into planning. They are a very useful resource for stimulating ideas for next steps for children who have shown interests or obsessions, for example fire engines or pirates. However, PLOD is a tool that excels when used for schema because, by definition, all the children in that group have at least one common interest – their schema. A PLOD may be more difficult to complete for a key group of children because all the children would have to share the same interests at the same time. There may be occasions when a group of children are interested in a superhero or zoo animals – after a trip, for example – when PLODs could be very useful (see Figure 5.1).

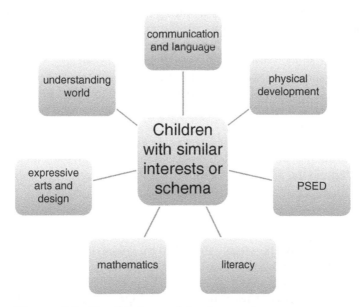

Figure 5.1   Possible lines of development

Example box

Peter Pan Pantomime Trip

A Christmas trip was planned to see the Peter Pan pantomime at the local theatre. All the practitioners had done lots of preparation, explaining how the crocodile and Captain Hook would be there, but so would Tinkerbell and Peter Pan. Different stories were read and the children started to incorporate key characters into their drawings and play.

After the Christmas break the children were still enthused about Peter Pan, asking for the climbing frame to be turned into the Lost Boys hideout. The practitioners realized there were still plenty of activities to support this shared interest, so developed a PLOD:

- Communication and language: investigating how pirates talk, pirate songs, retelling the story, creating new characters;
- Physical development: using the climbing frame hideout, having to climb to the top to get inside, playing 'follow the leader', with the children taking it in turns to play the Peter Pan leader;
- Personal, social and emotional development: working together as the Lost Boys; discussions, pictures and 3D models to show how different characters may be feeling (was the crocodile cross with Peter Pan or Captain Hook or just didn't like the clock's ticking?);
- Literacy: making own books about Peter Pan, alliteration (Peter Pan, Pirates Plan, Hook's Hideout);
- Expressive arts and design: Peter Pan hats, Tinkerbell wands, recreating the stage show, making up words to 'follow the leader';
- Understanding the world: talk about the different family groups/communities. The Lost Boys had a different family to Peter, Michael and Wendy. How might living on an island be different to living in your own town or village?
- Mathematical development: creating treasure maps and then making them 'for real' in the sand tray, mapping the maps onto the sand; repeat patterns in the 'red Indian's' headdress feathers and squaw's beads.

The PLOD method is closely linked to the areas of learning and development of the EYFS, so is best suited for Category 1: Child Development of the next steps categories. It would also be possible to formulate a PLOD where the EYFS areas of learning and development are substituted with the areas of continuous provision and how these could be used to support

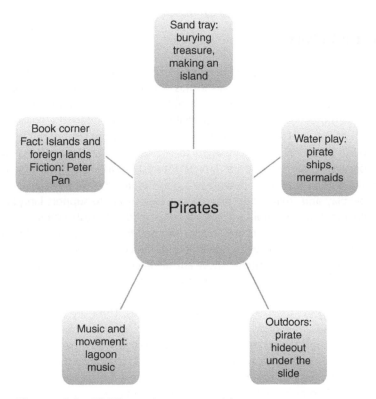

Figure 5.2 PLOD continuous provision

the children's development (see Figure 5.2). These should only be used for ideas, or starting points, for the next steps. Although they may generate many ideas, some may never be used because the child's children's interests will change.

The role of the adult

It is useful for practitioners to think about the role of the adults in next steps. Is it reinforcing and scaffolding, or stretching and challenging? This may determine how the practitioner does the activity and whether it is in a group or as an individual practitioner supporting a child. This will also vary from practitioner to practitioner. Different people have different ideas and bring varied life experiences to their setting. Some practitioners will naturally tend towards planning more challenging activities, while others may want to do more supportive activities.

Example box

At Goodwood Lodge, the practitioners have regular meetings where the next steps are discussed. Sharing ideas in this way means that the practitioners have an opportunity to see the next steps from a different point of view and to broaden their own knowledge. It enables them to explore the heart of a child's interests and not just jump to the first next step that is thought of.

The practitioners are encouraged to see the activities from the child's perspective, so a child who has limited interest in writing may be encouraged to 'sign in' with their parents as a non-threatening writing activity.

Role-play and small world play is used extensively to support language development, imagination and to make the child's interests visible. This is both indoors and outdoors and is not restricted to one area within the setting, but happens in all areas. For example, the Letters and Sounds framework is presented via a magic show and a practitioner plays the part of a 'mad witch' to explore numeracy with the children.

As part of their partnership commitment, parents receive a copy of their child's major next steps on a 3-month rolling basis. These are also displayed on the wall as a reminder to practitioners of the 'bigger picture'. There are activity ideas for parents to do with their children, for example, recognizing the traffic light colours or singing songs together in the car on the way home.

All these methods ensure that the practitioners are constantly thinking about the children's development and progress in a very positive way.

It is part of the practitioner's skill to determine which category (as described earlier in the chapter) to use for each child in each circumstance, i.e. child development, extend an interest, embed a learning point or personal, social and emotional development. There are no 'right' or 'wrong' answers. Two practitioners may make the same observation of a single child and develop completely different, but equally valid, next steps to meet that child's needs. This skill can be developed through practice and self-reflection.

Example box

While visiting a friend's nursery, I noticed one of the pre-school girls gluing 'jewels' around the side of a preformed box. She had decided to make an alternating pattern – diamond then ruby then diamond then ruby.

I was chatting later on to her key person, who said that the little girl was very creative. She was getting more confident with the glue stick and attempting more complex items. Her key person was going to follow this activity with some more creativity in the afternoon, introducing a greater variety of 'jewels' and colours.

Intrigued, I wondered what other practitioners in the setting might have chosen as a next step in this case. So I described the jewel gluing scenario to each practitioner individually and discussed some of the next steps. Interestingly, no two answers were exactly the same!

- One practitioner said she would extend this by getting the building blocks and doing 3D repeat patterns, taking this into a grid formation (x and y axes) eventually (mathematical development).
- Another practitioner said she would extend the creativity by including other craft materials as well as 'jewels' (expressive arts).
- A third practitioner said she would start a 'pattern hunt' looking outdoors for patterns in nature, such as sunflower heads, leaf veins and seed pods (creating and thinking critically).

When I discussed the difference in the answers, there was some surprise, because to each practitioner their own next step seemed the 'obvious' one. However, there was agreement that these were all valuable and effective next steps for the child's development.

Contingency

What happens if the 'next step' activity or idea doesn't work or the children don't engage with the ideas put forward?

Practitioners need to review and reflect when the children fail to engage meaningfully with the planned next steps. Could it be the place, time, group of friends who were there or because it involved sharing? Sometimes there is no easy answer, but it is worth taking the time to reflect on why some activities aren't as successful as they may be. This stops mistakes being repeated. Similarly, it is useful to note what the children decided to do instead of the planned activity. Did they subvert it in some way; for example, mix all the paints together instead of mixing just two colours, which had been the planned activity?

However, all may not be lost. Practitioners should also review the aim of the next step and whether this was still achieved, albeit not by the method envisaged. Taking the paint example again, if the aim of the activity was to explore mixing, then this has still been achieved with this activity. If the original activity was to specifically explore the colour changes when blue and red are mixed, then the activity could be deemed a 'failure'. However, is it important that the children know, at this point, the colour combinations, or is it more important that they understand that mixing paints together means the colour will change? They may not be ready to remember the colour combinations yet, but an enjoyment of the activity means they will return to it at a later date, with a mastery disposition and an eagerness to try mixing colours.

Practical considerations

There are some practical considerations in the recording of next steps. Should these be recorded after the assessment at the bottom of the activity sheet or should they be at the top of the activity sheet so that the aim of the activity is clearly displayed? Simply put, the answer is that it should be wherever the practitioners can make the best use of them. There is no point in writing thoughtful, thorough, useful next steps if they are not kept in mind when the activity is in progress.

Next steps should be shared with other practitioners working in the room, so everyone can effectively support all the children in their care. The key person has the responsibility of thoroughly knowing and understanding the next steps of their key children at all times.

Key learning points

Next steps must relate to the observation and assessment and can be categorized under four main areas: child development, extend an interest, embed a learning point and personal, social and emotional development. It must be clear what the role of the practitioner is in supporting the next steps and they must be practical. Effective next steps depend on practitioners really knowing and understanding their children and having reliable observations and assessments.

Reflective questions

1 Try the 'next steps experiment' in your setting. Describe a situation and ask each practitioner privately how they would extend the activity. The number of different ideas that are generated may surprise you.

2   Look through the next steps that you choose for your children. Consider:
   • Are they generally in the same area of learning and development?
   • Could you explore other areas of learning and development?
   • Do you allow opportunities for children to repeat activities?
3   Explain your next steps to a colleague or critical friend. Consider:
   • Can you explain which category of next step it is?
   • Do you favour one category over the others?
   • How could these be strengthened and expanded?
   • Have you considered the child's perspective?

Further reading

Worthington, M. and Carruthers, E. (2003) Research uncovers children's creative mathematical thinking, *Primary Mathematics (Mathematics Association)*, 7(3): 21–5.
Young children's creativity when doing maths is explored, including how mark making can give a visual analysis of children's thought processes. The research shows how maths worksheets fail to support mathematical learning and offers alternatives.

6   What is planning?

*It is children's learning which must be our main concern, not our plans
or schemes of work. They should support the learning, not hinder it.*

(Hutchin 2000: 9)

Chapter objectives

- To explore the different forms of planning
- To critically examine the purpose of planning

Chapter overview

Sometimes planning can just seem a chore that has to be done. Planning
shouldn't be like that, nor does it need to be. Planning should have an
aim, it should be purposeful. It should also be flexible and responsive to
the children's needs and for the benefit of children, practitioners and
families. Often the best planning systems are the simplest. However the
very best sort of planning is something that everybody understands, can
use and does use on a daily basis. The most beautiful planning systems are
of no use if practitioners do not use them, if they cannot be explained to
other practitioners, or if they cannot be explained to the Ofsted inspector.

In this chapter, concepts around planning are explored, such as long-,
medium- and short-term planning. Some of the definitions from the
EYFS are discussed and how these translate from statutory requirements
into practical requirements in this setting. Some of the planning methods and ideas from theorists are considered, along with parental involvement. Displaying planning in a meaningful way and the benefits and
challenges of free-flow play in terms of planning are also discussed.

Types of planning

In the past planning has been divided into neat categories called long-,
medium- and short-term planning. These had specific meanings, so that

long-term planning meant planning activities for the following year, medium-term plans were the planning for each term or half term and short-term planning consisted of the weekly planning sheets.

However, this strict routine of planning has on the whole been replaced with a more flexible, responsive system. Planning should be based around the needs and interests of the children attending the setting. This may necessitate planning on a daily basis to reflect the interests of the children who are attending that day. There is still some need for long-term planning, and even a small amount of medium-term planning, but the majority of planning should now be on a daily or possibly weekly basis. This is so the activities accurately reflect the children's interests at the time when they are current. A week in a young child's life is a long time, when ideas and fascinations may evaporate, and practitioners can lose the opportunity to capitalize on these. After all, there are so many interesting things happening all the time that it would be surprising to find a child still enthusiastic about finding a spider a week later.

We will now examine the different sorts of planning and reflect on how this has changed since the advent of the EYFS.

Long-term planning

Long-term planning was usually done over the summer holidays ready for the September intake. These plans were often in large A4 lever arch folders, where each half term's topic or theme had been decided months in advance. Sometimes these folders were reused from year to year, with the same themes or topics appearing in each half term.

Although this was very useful for ensuring that certain festivals or celebrations were acknowledged, these plans took no account of the children who would be attending the setting that year. In fact, for a lot of preschools, these were written before the children had even started attending the setting. With the current focus on child-led activities, following children's interests and reacting to the sorts of stimuli that children find interesting, these folders have largely become redundant. How can you predict what children may be interested in before you have even met them?

Of course some form of long-term planning is still needed. This will encompass information such as the dates of the Chinese New Year, Easter, Christmas, Eid, special celebrations at the nursery, charity events and holiday dates. There are some useful resources you can buy, or download from websites, which have all the dates of the festivals for each year as well as other information, such as which animal is represented for that Chinese New Year. The long-term plans may also include visits or visitors to the setting that need to be booked in advance, for example the

Fire Brigade. These may be necessary to coordinate with other settings or schools, or holidays and training days.

For some practitioners not having the security of long-term planning can be quite unsettling as they like the certainty of knowing what is coming next. They enjoy looking forward to the topics coming up, finding resources and discussing this with the children. The worry about the preparation of equipment and resources is a valid one. When planning topics or themes in advance the resources that are required are already known in advance, whereas if you are following the children's interests, gathering together resources may have to be done at very short notice. A lot of the workload can be reduced by having boxes of resources that you are likely to need. For example, it is likely that the children will have an interest in dinosaurs, pirates or snow at some time during the year. Boxes holding resources pertinent to these topics can be kept to one side. These may include things like dressing up equipment, books, posters or ice cube trays. Ideas for activities associated with these interests can also be included, such as games, useful websites or photos of children previously playing with the activities to spark ideas.

However, for other practitioners the lack of long-term planning is quite freeing and they like that they will not know what they will be doing next half term. Instead they will be listening to the children's interests and will be able to use their own creativity to plan meaningful experiences for the children.

Medium-term planning

Medium-term planning is the planning of events that may be happening in the next month or so. There is not so much need for medium-term planning under the EYFS, although there may be times when it is useful. This may include the imminent arrival of a baby sibling, a trip out or a visitor to the setting, for example. Medium-term planning can be used very effectively to plan the environment. This may be as simple as use of the outdoors during the summer or maybe the inclusion of new resources.

Short-term planning

Most of the planning under the EYFS is done in the short term. This means different things to different settings, from planning a week in advance to a few hours in advance. It should always be responsive and flexible, changing to suit the children's needs at that time. Practitioners should be reflective and consider how each activity is progressing, making adjustments as necessary.

There are many ways of recording short-term planning. One popular method is the 'cheese wedge' method: activities are planned in full for the whole of the first day; a few activities are planned for the second day, with maybe one or two activities planned for the third day. The fourth and fifth days are left blank. So, looking at the planning on the planning sheets, it looks like a cheese wedge, with the thick end being closest chronologically.

During the first day activities would be entered into the planning ready for the second day. These may be activities that the children have enjoyed, or ideas that have been sparked from activities during that day. This is repeated for each day, so that planning is completed on a rolling daily basis. The beauty of this method is that it is immediately responsive to the children's interest at that time. It can also demonstrate personalized planning, by adding the children's name or initials next to the activity. The ideas are fresh in the practitioners' minds.

Suggestions for activities suitable for a particular group of children, for example children that only attend on certain days, can be put on the planning in advance.

If the activity doesn't work as well as expected, or the children themselves change it, or the children are interested in something else that day, then the planning sheet is simply altered by putting a line through the activity and writing in the replacement activity. This demonstrates flexibility and being responsive to the children's interests. It can also be useful to write in the reasons why this activity didn't work. For example, it could be doing finger paints with a group of younger 2-year-old boisterous boys wasn't very successful due to the age of this particular group of children. In this example it would be useful to write on the planning 'boys didn't engage with this activity, consider doing it as a small group instead' or 'this group would respond to a more physical activity in this morning session'.

Similarly, making comments on the planning as to why or how activities worked well can be very useful for future planning. This could be very simple, such as 'loved the glitter' or 'enjoyed this CD'. By using this information, practitioners are more likely to choose resources or ideas that match the children's interests.

Short-term planning sheets may also include a range of other information, as well as the actual activities. This could include:

- resources required for the activity;
- physical area where the activity is to take place (e.g. outdoors, sand tray, construction area);

- staff involved with the activity;
- areas linking to the EYFS;
- links with home;
- next steps all follow-on activities;
- evaluation of the activity.

Short-term planning should be displayed somewhere in the room, easily accessible by all practitioners, so that everyone is aware of the plans for the day. This also means that practitioners can update and modify planning quickly and easily. Everybody should be encouraged to participate in the planning process so they have ownership of the activities in the room. It also ensures that practitioners are able to plan for each of their key children. Encouraging practitioners to review and alter the planning accordingly is a good way to encourage reflective practice.

Planning of continuous provision

Continuous provision activities are those activities that are out all the time. This may be the sand tray, water tray, construction blocks, dressing up or home corner. The children can access these at all times during the session and they are out every day. The planning of continuous provision should be done when there is a perceived need. It is usually when a practitioner notices that an area is not being used or is not being used to its full potential that the continuous provision is reviewed.

This can vary greatly from setting to setting. Pack-away settings, for example, have to be set up anew every day. In a day nursery, the continuous provision may not change for many months which could result in children getting bored with the same activities. To prevent this, practitioners should endeavour to enhance the continuous provision constantly. This can be as simple as putting new toys in the sand tray, or putting floating and sinking objects in the water tray.

Information box

Facilitating child-initiated learning

One of the first worries about the EYFS when it was published in 2007 was the concept of child-initiated play. What did it mean and how would you 'plan' for child-initiated play when the children are leading the play?

Similarly the EYFS (DfE 2012b) calls for a 'purposeful play and . . . a mix of adult led and child-initiated activity' (p. 6), but falls short of defining 'child-initiated'.

Jennie Lindon (2008) summarizes child-initiated events as 'children choose freely from their learning environment – indoors and out – and select and organise resources, picking their own companions on the way' (p. 14).

In the strict sense of the word you can't 'plan' for the activity that is in a child's mind. But you can plan the environment and experience to facilitate this. For example, you can have open-ended resources such as lengths of fabric and cardboard boxes available, that the children can access easily (indoors and outdoors), empowering them to play in the areas they would prefer.

There may be occasions when you can anticipate the type of resources that the children would enjoy. If you have a child with a strong schematic play such as transporting, you can provide bags, prams, trolleys and dumper trucks.

Practitioner's role

The practitioner's role is to be supportive and encouraging. Moyles states that the practitioner needs to be 'playful and flexible, but [have] specific, knowledgeable and excellent communication skills' (2008: 35). In many respects this is much more skilful and demanding than pre-planning a 'learning experience' and then leading the children through the taught session. It means that you are a facilitator in the child's play, responding to their prompts and lead. This needs to be done respectfully and thoughtfully. There is a big difference between being invited to a tea party and gate-crashing it!

What should your response be if the child-initiated play is concerning? If you think it is a potential safeguarding issue, such as play with an overtly sexual theme, then the safeguarding policies and procedures must be followed. If the play is that the boys are making guns out of Lego or that the latest superhero is prevalent in their games, then you must decide on a setting-wide approach. Penny Holland's seminal book *We Don't Play with Guns Here* (2003) explains how supporting this type of play in a controlled manner can support imaginative play and social development and may be used as a platform to reach 'hard-to-manage children' (p. 78).

Planning for every child

It can be quite a daunting task to think that you have to plan for every child in a room of 12 or a class of 30! However, this can be achieved in a number of ways.

Multiple aspects of one activity

One activity may satisfy the needs and interests of many different children. For example the activity may be dinosaurs in the sand tray. This would be interesting for children who like to find hidden objects under the sand; children who like small world role-playing; children who like dinosaurs; children who like pouring and tipping sand and children who like burying objects. So in this one simple activity five different children could each have their needs met. Practitioners do need to be aware of how the activity is meeting their children's needs and be able to support this with suitable scaffolding. This could be use of language, demonstrating play or provoking responses ('what do you think would happen if we did...?').

Grouping of children

Think carefully about how you can group the children together. It may be useful to group those who have similar interests, for example schema (see PLODs in Chapter 5). The planning should include resources to support the schema, suitable activities and provocations.

Example box

Colette, Liam, Charlotte and Ben all display transporting schema play.

Resources: The planning includes plenty of open-ended transporting equipment, such as handbags, picnic baskets, trolleys and buckets.
Activity: In addition the practitioners have set up a 'postman's round' with post boxes set up around the setting. During the day the children can put letters into the post boxes. It is the 'postman's' job to collect the mail from each box and hand out the letters.
Provocation: Sometimes there are really big parcels – how are we going to carry these? Can you find a big enough bag? Sometimes the parcels are very heavy – will this need two people to carry it?

Children could be grouped in mixed ages and/or abilities, to encourage peer support and peer-to-peer learning. The practitioner's role is to model interactions, support learning and encourage cooperation. The practitioner gives individualized support to each child, offering more or less support as required. For example, the practitioner may let more able children climb the climbing frame by themselves, but would give more support to a less confident or less able child.

Making planning accessible to all

The planning for any room or child should be understood by and accessible to all practitioners. This means that planning should be included as part of staff induction, even if the member of staff is in the room temporarily, and should not be 'something the room manager does'. The reason for this is that practitioners have to understand not only *what* to do, but also *why*. So the bubbles in the water tray may be to support the language development of one child, gross motor skills of another and creative development of a third child. Once the practitioner knows this they can support the children in an appropriate manner. Accessible planning can be accomplished by having regular staff meetings to discuss the current planning. These do not need to be formal, recorded meetings, but could be a 10-minute get together so that everyone understands what is on the planning sheet for the next few days.

Invariably Ofsted inspectors will ask to see a sample of planning, and maybe how it fits with a child's learning journey or why these particular activities have been chosen. Hence, it is essential that all practitioners are able to explain how the observations, next steps, children's interests and personalized provision are represented on the planning.

Parents could also be part of the planning process, fostering true parent partnership, helping to suggest activities that their child enjoys, for example. Whalley (2007) suggests that parents should be engaged as 'decision-makers in the planning and implementation' (p. 4) of childcare at the setting. At the very least, it is good practice to give parents and carers access to the planning, so they can appreciate the sorts of things their child may be enjoying at the setting. If the setting's planning is reasonably complicated, or has lots of early years jargon, it may be worth displaying a simplified version. Further details could then be discussed with parents as questions arise.

Other approaches to planning

HighScope

HighScope's approach to early childhood education emphasizes 'active participatory learning'. Children's interests and choices are at the heart of HighScope programmes and active learning means children have direct, hands-on experiences with people, objects, events and ideas. HighScope classrooms all have a daily routine, which has been specifically tailored to meet the needs of the particular class (HighScope 2012). There will always be six elements:

Plan-do-review

This is the element that most practitioners will recognize as being at the core of the HighScope philosophy. It starts with a small group where the children nominate what they play with, with whom, etc. The children may be taken around the room or setting first to see the type of activities that are available for them. Once decided, the children are free to play for between 45 minutes and an hour on their chosen activities. Then they come together again to review their learning during the session. The children are able to change their 'plan' during the play session, according to their interests. They are expected to tidy up after themselves and keep the activities tidy during the day.

Small-group time

A small group of children, usually the key children group, have an adult-led or adult-initiated activity. The children are free to take the activity in any direction they feel interested in and the activities are planned to support and challenge the children's thinking.

Large-group time

These are typically story time, music and movement and group art.

Outside time

There is always an opportunity to go outside and experience the outdoors. Appreciation of nature is actively encouraged.

Transition times

These are the times of day when the child arrives at the setting and leaves the setting and the time between activities. Children are encouraged to make their own choices about how transitions occur so the children have control over their environment and decision-making, for example how they transition from large group time to going outdoors.

Eating and resting times

These are designed to reflect routines at the child's home, wherever possible.

Independence, self-esteem and decision-making are fostered in the way that the children have the ability to plan their own activities. The HighScope teachers plan and evaluate the day's activities as a team and are expected to develop a philosophy of education with child development at its centre (Roopnarine and Johnson 2008). A criticism of the HighScope philosophy is that the plan-do-review can be too structured and there is limited time for child-initiated play (Miller and Pound 2011).

Montessori

The Montessori approach is characterized by an emphasis on independence, freedom and respect for the child. Components of an authentic Montessori include multi-age groupings that foster peer learning, uninterrupted blocks of work time, and guided choice of work activity together with specially designed Montessori learning materials. Planning in a Montessori environment is much less formalized. The plans follow the needs and interests of the children on that day, so sometimes there may be small group work, and sometimes not. The Montessori approach is summed up as 'plans rather than programmes' (Montessori Education 2012). There is equipment and resources to support all areas of learning and development and the children are encouraged by the Montessori teacher in the areas that the teacher thinks the child needs (Jones 2005).

Isaacs

Susan Isaacs set up the Malting House School in 1924, where the emphasis was on 'children's curiosity, their emotional needs and on the importance of language' (Pound 2005: 32). The children's ages ranged from 2 to 8 years. At the school there were no formal lessons planned; children were free to choose to access any area of learning they wanted to investigate. Although there was no formal planning of activities or lessons, the environment was planned to support the children's learning and was designed to be an emotionally secure place. Although children had the freedom to choose their activities, there were clear behavioural boundaries that children had to respect.

Monitoring planning

If you are in a small setting, or a childminder, it is relatively easy to monitor yourself and keep planning relevant and up to date. However, if you are part of a larger team it may be necessary to have formal monitoring systems in place. It is likely that part of every practitioner's job description will be to do planning, keep it up to date and display it appropriately. Similarly, the room manager's role should involve an element of monitoring and the setting manager can do spot checks to support this.

Example box

'Sunshine' preschool had been using the same planning sheets for over a year. The practitioners were familiar with them and they were used productively.

However, last September the nursery started admitting 2-year-olds for the first time. The practitioners found that the planning wasn't meeting the needs of their youngest children. The activities didn't seem to engage them; circle time was disrupted; toys ended up all over the nursery.

When they reviewed the planning it was found that the time planned for circle time was far too long; the activities were more suitable to the older age group and that tidy up time had not been explained thoroughly to their new children.

The planning was altered so that circle time was very brief for the younger children but full length as before for the older children. The settling in time also now includes lots of support and modelling from the practitioners for tidy up time, behaviour and accessing resources.

Final thoughts

Planning is intended to support children's development, and as a tool to help practitioners ensure they are meeting the needs of the children. As with any tool, it should only be used in the right circumstances. If there is a fall of snow, or a baby is brought into the setting, or a child comes back after a particularly exciting trip at the weekend, then this must take priority over the 'planned' activities. Planning should be flexible and responsive, working for the benefit of the children, not the children working to the planning. This can be frustrating for practitioners, but it is essential to meet the children's needs before the planning requirements. Planning can always be kept to be used another day.

Planning depends on good quality, regular observations and assessments. Making this part of the ethos of the setting is essential, so it is seen as adding value to the practitioner's work and valuable for the children's development. With this in mind, staff should have regular training on the setting's observation, assessment and planning systems, especially as the systems grow and evolve. The induction of new staff must include detailed instructions on the observation, assessment and planning methods, to ensure that bad habits are not accidentally introduced. Where there may be problems, such as practitioners who may have dyslexia or a lack of confidence or practitioners with English as an additional language, the practitioner should be supported and helped, rather than being left to struggle or omitted from doing observations.

Key learning points

Long-term planning and short-term planning are the most commonly used elements within early years. Long-term planning provides for an overview of the year with, for example, fixed dates for festivals. Short-term planning reflects the particular interests and needs of the children at that time, and must be responsive, on a daily basis, to the changes in children's ideas. It is paramount that planning reflects individual children's needs, to ensure personalized provision.

Reflective questions

1   How do you ensure that every child's needs are met in your planning system? Consider:
   • Could every practitioner say what is planned for their key child that day?
   • Are there clear reasons for why this activity was chosen?
2   Are the multiple aspects of one activity utilized by practitioners? Consider:
   • How do practitioners know all the different ways that an activity can support the different areas of learning and development?
   • Are there prompt sheets around the setting to remind practitioners of vocabulary to use and questions to ask?
   • How do you monitor this?
3   Does your induction process include introductions to the planning system? Consider:
   • How do practitioners learn about planning?
   • What support is available to each person?
   • Could collaboration between rooms or a childminding network strengthen the planning system?

Further reading

Classic research

Montessori, M. (2008) *Dr Montessori's Own Handbook*. Radford: Wilder.
This is a great introduction to the Montessori method.
Graham, P. (2008) *Susan Isaacs: A Life Freeing the Minds of Children*.
    London: Karnac Books.
Philip Graham's book gives a context and biographical details of Susan
Isaac's life.
You will have to remember the time and cultures that these were written.
Compare these with practice today. How much is similar and how much
has changed? What can we learn from these?

Contemporary research

Dunphy, E. (2010) Assessing early learning through formative assessment:
    key issues and considerations, *Irish Educational Studies*, 29(1): 41–56.
Dunphy investigated formative assessment, methods and challenges. In
this paper, she discusses the practitioner's role, aspects of learning and
approaches to assessment.
Maynard, T., Waters, J. and Clement, J. (2011) Moving outdoors: further
    explorations of 'child-initiated' learning in the outdoor environ-
    ment, *Education 3–13: International Journal of Primary, Elementary and
    Early Years Education*: 1–18.
http://www.tandfonline.com/doi/abs/10.1080/03004279.2011.578750
    (accessed 18 November 2012).
In this research the authors aim to 'identify whether, and if so how,
teachers' practice differed when supporting child-initiated/centred learning outdoors compared with their 'normal' classroom practice' (p. 2). It
contains some interesting discussion about practitioners' views of the different types of learning, linked with the Reggio Emilia approach.

7   Planning for the EYFS using assessments

In planning and guiding children's activities, practitioners must reflect on the different ways that children learn and reflect these in their practice.

(DfE 2012b: 6)

Chapter objectives

- To consider some specific planning techniques
- To discuss some practical issues when writing planning
- To bring together the observation, assessment and planning cycle

Chapter overview

This chapter explores the different ways in which planning may be linked to observations and assessments in the EYFS. Every setting will have its own unique, evolving method, which the practitioner will need to be able to use and understand. However, there are some rules of general good practice that practitioners need to be aware of. Some of the challenges are also considered here.

Introduction

There are a number of key documents that are likely to heavily influence your approach to planning: the EYFS; Development Matters and the Ofsted inspection regime.

EYFS Statutory Framework (2012)

In the revised EYFS a 'secure foundation' (DfE 2012b: 2) is underpinned by planning learning and development opportunities. It is statutory that practitioners 'plan a challenging and enjoyable experience for each child in all areas of learning and development' and that these are implemented through 'planned, purposeful play' (p. 6). Planning is explicitly linked to assessment on page 10, where practitioners are also told to develop 'targeted' plans to support children with SEN.

The Foundation Stage Profile should be used to help plan activities for Year 1, including those children with special educational needs or disabilities, although 'reasonable adjustments to the assessment process for children with special educational needs and disabilities must be made as appropriate' (p. 12).

Development Matters (2012)

Planning for children's learning and development runs throughout the Development Matters guidance, published by Early Education, and is represented by the two columns 'positive relationships' and 'enabling environments'. This is summed up very neatly on page 7 of the 'creating and thinking critically' characteristic of effective learning: 'In planning activities, ask yourself: *Is this an opportunity for children to find their own ways to represent and develop their own ideas?* Avoid children just reproducing someone else's ideas.'

Ofsted inspection (2012)

The inspection regime for England, under Ofsted, has been re-evaluated to meet the needs of the revised EYFS. There is now a move away from providing paper work as evidence of good practice, with the main evidence being 'direct observations of care practices, children's behaviour and their interactions with practitioners and each other' (Ofsted 2012: 10). This can be supplemented by evidence of written planning, although to achieve a grade of 'Good' planning and assessment must be 'monitored to make sure they are consistent, precise, and display an accurate understanding of all children's skills, abilities and progress' (p. 14).

Commercial planning systems

There are a number of commercially available observation, assessment and planning systems. These should not be seen as a quick fix or the solution to all problems. The system must be suited to your setting, for example a planning system designed for a large, multi-room setting is unlikely to be suitable for a childminder or nanny. The critical part of any system is how the different parts mesh together. Practitioners must understand how each part of the observation, assessment and planning cycle operate within the system.

Planning in the EYFS

As you are probably now aware, the revised EYFS has three prime areas:

1   personal, social and emotional development;
2   communication and language;
3   physical development;

with four specific areas:

1   literacy;
2   mathematics;
3   understanding the world;
4   expressive arts and design.

The prime and specific areas of learning are from the recommendations made by Dame Tickell in her review of the EYFS in 2011 *The Early Years: Foundations for Life, Health and Learning.* Tickell based her decisions on how to split the areas of learning and development on neuroscience research by John Hall. Hall (2005) explains how there are two different sorts of learning – 'experience expectant' and 'experience dependent' (p. 16). Experience expectant learning is learning that humans have evolved to expect, for example using the five senses. Having the tactile experience of our environment around us 'teaches' the brain how to respond to the environment. For example, the pain of touching a hot coal will make us more wary of being near the fire. These experiences mean we can respond to stimuli appropriately. Experience dependent learning is culturally driven or arises from a social necessity. For example, the brain has an 'evolutionary imperative' (Hall 2005: 16) towards speech (experience expectant) but not towards reading, which is a demand made by the society and culture within which we live (experience dependent).

Based on this research, Tickell (2011) has named the experience expectant areas of learning the prime areas and the experience dependent areas of learning the specific areas. For this reason the 'literacy' part of Communication, Language and Literacy in the original EYFS has been moved to the specific area, because it is a cultural and societal area of learning and development. Importantly, Tickell concluded that the three prime areas are interdependent and 'represent the earliest stages of development' (Tickell 2011: 92) and that the relationship between the prime and specific areas of learning is 'not chronological but symbiotic; the prime areas are necessary but not sufficient' (p. 96).

Personal, social and emotional development

Personal, social and emotional development is widely accepted as under-pinning any child's development. Dowling (2010) suggests that it opens the doors for 'a life of personal fulfilment whatever their other achieve-ments' (p. 8). In her report on the revised EYFS, Dame Tickell states that 'starting the process of successful personal, social and emotional develop-ment is essential for young children in all aspects of their lives' (Tickell 2011: 93). Conversely, Perry and Szalavitz (2008) describe how 'cata-strophic events can leave indelible marks on the mind . . . the impact is actually far greater in children than it is on adults' (p. 2). For these rea-sons it is vitally important that observations, assessment and planning take full account of personal, social and emotional development.

Example box

Observation:

Harry was playing with his friends when one of them snatched a toy. Harry said, 'We must share our toys. We have kind hands'.

Assessment:

Harry is aware of the behaviour rules of the setting (kind hands) and under-stands that snatching toys breaks those rules.

Next steps:

Support Harry's knowledge of the behaviour rules and give encouragement to continue to express these.

Planning:

Reinforce the behavioural rules with all the children, either at small group time, key person time or circle time.

Physical development

Children naturally like to move and explore their surroundings with their whole body. It is an essential part of getting to know their environ-ment and also developing a range of skills. For example, using your body and 'teaching' your brain to understand where your arms and legs are will develop proprioception (knowing the orientation of your own body in space). This is the skill that enables you to tie an apron behind your back, which you can only do with practice. Children who have sensory integration difficulties find it hard to isolate and move individual parts of the body. White (2008) maintains that children learn 'most effectively through doing and moving' (p. 70) and that observation and assessments must be made outside as well, because children 'react differently to the spaces and experiences available' (p. 11).

Example box

Ayres and Robbins (2005) suggest you try this exercise, which simulates how a child with poor proprioception may feel:

- Take off your socks so you have bare feet.
- Close your eyes and ask a friend to touch one of your middle toes.
- Which one was touched?
- Was it difficult to guess, or could you link the touch with the correct toe?

Many people find this difficult because we rarely have to use our toes individually, as we do our fingers, so the brain doesn't readily identify them individually. Children who have sensory integration problems will not be able to identify an individual finger, just as you may not have been able to identify a toe.

Example box

Observation:

Nick is confident when climbing the steps up to the back door and the steps on the small slide outside. He does use the handrail, but only occasionally, to steady himself.

Assessment:

Nick has good gross motor skills and coordination, but is still coming up the steps one at a time.

Next steps:

To encourage Nick to use alternate feet when going up the stairs.

Planning:

Ensure that all practitioners know that Nick is trying to use alternate feet on the stairs, so everyone can encourage and support him.

Communication and language

It is likely that you will have many observations of communication and language, whatever age range you work with. Babies communicate from birth, using 'protoconversations' (David et al. 2005: 47), with their language becoming more sophisticated as they mature. Most activities are enhanced by use of a rich and varied language, sharing ideas and using sustained shared thinking. The EYFS (DfE 2012b) states that, when assessing children whose home language is not English, practitioners must still assess their skills in English, but also 'explore the child's skills in the home language with parents and/or carers' (p. 6).

Example box

Observation:

Alice talked about her visit to her Grandma's and how she had seen the new kittens. She had explained how kitten are baby cats.

Assessment:

Alice gave a clear chronological account of the day at her Grandma's, demonstrating good knowledge about baby animals growing up. Her vocabulary is good for her age (30 months) using lots of describing words such as furry, soft, cuddly.

Next steps:

Extend Alice's language through supported role play of kittens.

Use fact book about cats.

Display photos on the gallery of Alice with the kittens.

Planning:

Discuss having a 'pet's corner' in the home corner, using Alice's pictures.

Display the vocabulary on the continuous provision sheets in the home corner, to encourage practitioners to extend language.

Literacy

Literacy has been taken out of the communication, language and literacy area of learning and development and is now a standalone, in the specific area rather than the prime area. This recognizes the concern of many practitioners that putting the same emphasis on literacy as on a child's communication skills meant that many children were being encouraged to read and write at an inappropriate stage in their lives. Whitehead (2004) maintains that early literacy is about 'sharing and negotiating meanings through the use of sounds, words, images, gestures, objects and signs' (p. 206). Phonics is at the heart of the EYFS literacy, although sight-reading and writing of irregular words forms part of the ELG (Early Education 2012: 31).

Example box

Observation:

Matt is singing along to 'See-saw Marjary Daw'. He knows nearly all the words and is watching his key person intently as she sings.

Assessment:

Matt is enjoying the rhythm and rhyme, particularly with his key person.

Next steps:

Physical development: moving in rhythm to music

Outdoor play: using the see-saw while singing, full body movement for proprioception.

Creative arts: more complex songs

Planning:

Plan a music and movement session on a day that Matt attends. Ensure his key person is available to be with him.

Mathematics

Mathematical development is so much more than just 'numbers'. There are practitioners who will say that they are 'no good at maths', but can tell the time, stack and order boxes in the cupboards with pinpoint accuracy and know exactly how much milk to put in the jug for 12 thirsty children. These are all mathematical abilities that children learn while playing in all areas of the setting, from pouring water to carrying a handbag to exploring repeat patterns when sticking shapes onto a box. Observations should reflect all the different facets of mathematical development.

Example box

Observation:

Billy was putting all the big blocks into the pram. He put in as many as he could, squeezing the smaller blocks down the sides of the pram and balancing others on top. He tried pushing the pram, but found it was very heavy, so took some of the blocks from the top and tried again. This time he was successful, wheeling the blocks outdoors.

Assessment:

Billy showed good spatial awareness and demonstrated that he understood that he needed to take blocks off to make the pram lighter.

Next steps:

Explore putting the blocks into other containers; especially irregular shapes such as bags, so Billy can experiment with putting different sized blocks in to fill the space.

Investigate the weight of items the same size.

Planning:

Put the dressing up trolley next to the construction area, so the handbags and other bags are close for filling with blocks.

Adult-led activity: construct a tin full of pennies and an identical tin full of tissue paper. The children must guess which will be heavier and why. The practitioner's role is to encourage the children to carry and lift items, to find their weight compared to size.

Understanding the world

The very early aspects of understanding the world are closely linked to attachment, personal, social and emotional development (PSED) and communication and language. After all a baby's understanding of the world is going to be a very small circle encompassing his or her nearest and dearest. Children's views of the world change and develop as they grow up and interact with increasingly wider social systems (Bronfenbrenner 1979). This is reflected in Development Matters ELGs where children 'talk about the features of their own immediate environment and how environments might vary from one another' (p. 40).

Example box

Observation:

While making cards Liberty said 'I don't have birthday cards, do I?'
The practitioner asked 'Why do you think that is?'
'Because I have a different sort of birthday, with my mum and dad'.
'Do you know anyone else like that?'
'All my family!'

Assessment:

Liberty is becoming aware of her own culture as a Jehovah's Witness and how this differs from other cultures and communities. She has some understanding of what these differences are and is confident to talk about these.

Next steps:

Encourage Liberty to share information about her culture and bring in artifacts to share, where possible.

Planning:

Research the Jehovah's Witness calendar to find any significant dates.
Key person to liaise with the family to discuss their cultural needs.

Expressive arts and design

Expressive arts and design describes this area of learning and development more accurately than creative development (DfES 2008), which was often mistaken for craft type activities. In the revised EYFS it is made clear that children express their creativity in many ways, from dance and music to model-making and stories. Children's thinking is made visible through these activities and the process should be carefully observed, not just the finished 'product'. When talking about the famous Reggio Emilia philosophy of early childhood education, Hall et al. (2010) describe how 'Reggio teachers observe what the children are interested in and intrigued by, and they look to see how they can prolong this interest' (p. 36).

Example box

Observation:

When playing with the treasure basket, Milly (10 months old) was taking a great interest in the texture of the items, stroking the silky fabric and scrunching the foil. She spent a long time feeling the objects before picking them up. Occasionally she would bring an object to her mouth.

Assessment:

Milly is exploring textures in the world around her, using her whole body.

Next steps:

Explore further textures with Milly, in her environment, both indoors and outdoors.

Re-present the treasure baskets to embed the feeling of the textures.

Support with a wide variety of language and vocabulary, such as scrunchy, scratchy, soft, fluffy, etc.

Planning:

Present treasure baskets to the babies on an afternoon when Milly is in nursery. When outside, make her aware of the feel of the grass, gravel, leaves, etc.

Planning for specific situations

There are some times when planning may need special thought.

Key children

If you are lucky enough to be a key person to a group of children, you will almost certainly be expected to observe, assess and plan for them. This may be an easy task because these are the children you will know the most about, for whom you will know the families and will certainly see during the day. This also means that there is an expectation that you will complete more detailed, specific plans for these children and may even have to fill out regular progress checks (assessments) for the setting and/or the parents.

Sporadic attendance

There may be children in your setting who have sporadic attendance, for example children from travelling families or children from families who have a chaotic lifestyle caused by substance abuse. These can be particularly hard to plan for because the observations and assessments will be 'out of date' by the next time the child attends. Observations should be kept whenever possible and assessed as for other children. Ensure some time is put aside to do observations when the child does attend and discuss the child's development with parents and carers, including how development may be further supported at home.

One way to manage observation, assessment and planning for sporadic attendance is to create a personalized long-term plan, using information from parents or carers and initial assessment. This information is used to highlight the most critical areas for development, which are recorded and can be picked up when the child next returns to the setting. Progress is tracked against child development norms and Development Matters, but it must be remembered that progress may be delayed because there may be a period of 're-settling' each time the child attends. This must be sensitively conveyed to parents and carers, with even the smallest achievement recorded and celebrated.

Example box

Eli, 9 months, only attends nursery once a week and spends the rest of the week at home with his mum. It took him a long time to settle in the baby room, wanting to be carried and held at all times. It was identified at this stage that his most important need was to socialize with other children and to build up his self-confidence. After a number of weeks he was secure enough to play on the rug with the toys with the other children, as long as an adult was in close reach.

However, after a long break over the summer holidays, Eli was very clingy again and not interested in playing with the other children. His key person had a long chat with his mum, to reassure her that Eli would settle in again and to find any information that may help her match Eli's interests. Because socialization and self-confidence had already been identified as areas to prioritize, his key person was able to immediately focus on encouraging Eli to join in with the other children in messy play. At the end of the day Eli's key person took time to speak to mum and explain the sorts of things that Eli had done during the day, making sure she emphasized all his achievements.

Being able to monitor progress becomes impossible if assessment fails to take place at the setting and in schools due to sporadic attendance. Wilkin et al. (2010) highlighted this in their report into improving outcomes for Gypsy, Roma and Traveller pupils. In the report they state that 52 per cent of Gypsy, Roma and Traveller pupils were not assessed at Key Stage 1 (around 7 years old) so a 'progress score could not be calculated' (p. 9). Therefore, for just over half of this ethnic population, the effectiveness of the setting's observation, assessment and planning could not be measured, including any intervention programmes that had been implemented.

Shy or quiet children

It is important not to overlook those children who are quiet or shy. Techniques such as sustained shared thinking can be used effectively when there is time for one to one conversations. You may need to observe from a distance, so as not to interrupt play, or buddy the child with a more confident peer to support them in the setting.

Mixed age rooms

Managing rooms where children have a significant age gap (12 months or more) brings its own pleasures and challenges. In Sweden it is common practice to group children into toddlers (1–3 years old) and siblings (1–5 years old) (Samuelsson and Sheridan 2009) but it is less common in England. Children in nursery settings are usually in rooms with children of a similar age and developmental stage. Theoretically this should make observations easier, because the children are at similar stages. However, this can also make practitioners complacent and lead to them not challenging or stretching children, because they are within developmental norms. In mixed age rooms, or family rooms, each child must be considered as an individual because they will all be at different stages.

Childminders may have children where there is a wide age range, but with fewer children per adult. This means that childminders need to be conversant with child development across all the age ranges.

Key learning points

Using observations to determine next steps and using these in planning requires knowledge of both the child and child development. The examples given demonstrate how this can be achieved. There may be challenges, but these can be met with some thought and creativity.

Reflective questions

1   Is your planning process efficient or do you rewrite (copy out) observations and assessments unnecessarily?
2   Does each piece of paper 'work hard', i.e. does each piece of writing have at least two uses? For example, is an observation used to inform planning and then included in the child's folder? Are photographs used in displays then used as part of the planning folder?
3   Are parents really an integrated part of the planning process or are they passive observers? How can you involve parents with planning?
4   Can all staff members explain their planning, making clear links to observation and assessment? How could this be improved?

Further reading

Warash, B., Curtis, R., Hursh, D. and Tucci, V. (2008) Skinner meets Piaget on the Reggio playground: practical synthesis of applied behavior analysis and developmentally appropriate practice orientations, *Journal of Research in Childhood Education*, 22(4): 441–53.
In this intriguingly entitled paper, Warash et al. investigate how different practices, if developmentally appropriate, can be integrated into the pre-school environment, to support children to meet, or exceed, their developmental target.

PART THREE

Bringing it all together

8 Observations, assessment and planning for children with special educational needs

Effective observations and assessments should continue as an ongoing, cyclical process to ensure the most appropriate provision is made available to our youngest, and perhaps most vulnerable, children. If early identification is viewed as essential, then observations and assessments should be deemed equally as essential.

(Wall 2011: 141)

Chapter objectives

- To review the whole observe, assess and plan cycle in terms of children who may have SEN
- To bring together the specific requirements of SEN on the observation, assessment and planning cycle

Chapter overview

When observing children with SEN, there may be a different emphasis on the observations. In this chapter, some of the most common scenarios and the ways that the observation, assessment and planning cycle may have to be adapted to meet these needs are discussed. Clearly it is desirable that SEN are not viewed as a separate issue rather that all children will have their individual needs met, with SEN being just one part of a child's individuality, just as blue eyes or an interest in airplanes is now. Wall (2011) urges practitioners to observe the child, not the difficulties.

The biggest difference with these sorts of observations is the audience. As well as sharing observations with parents, carers and children they will be shared with a multi-professional team, possibly other key persons and other settings. This means that the observations may have to be more detailed and the context explained more explicitly. For example, an observation may note that the activity took place in the construction area, which is acceptable for practitioners who understand where the construction area is, but may mean nothing to an outside professional who does not know the layout of the setting.

This isn't to say that the observation, assessment and planning cycle is different throughout; there will also be some similarities. Observations will still be based on the individual child, wherever they happen to be in their development at that time. Wall (2011: 118) notes, 'whether the child's starting point is above or below the majority of children is irrelevant'. An assessment or evaluation of the observation will still be made, although this may be jointly with the multi-agency team. The planning of any activities resulting from this will still need to be incorporated into the setting's planning.

Sharing observations with parents

Parents and carers of children with special needs are more likely to be tuned in to their individual child's development and individual needs, especially if they have been closely involved with health professionals already. Practitioners should make use of this and ensure that parents' and carers' views are always included in the observation, assessment and planning cycle. Both Wall (2010) and Whalley (2007) recommend doing this during a home visit. This is particularly important for children with special needs because there may well be discussion points that parents would prefer to keep confidential or may find it hard to talk about.

Example box

Ben is a boisterous, happy 4½-year-old. He has some areas of delay, which are being addressed by practitioners in the setting. One of these areas is toilet training. Ben is due to start school in a few months but is still in nappies. Ben's mum, in particular, is very sensitive to this issue.

When the time comes to hand over the learning journeys, Ben's key person asks if she can do this as a home visit, so she can discuss how to approach Ben's individual needs ready for school. This gives them privacy to discuss toilet training and talking to the school and allows Ben's mum to freely express her concerns.

Observations will be the basis for any play plans, individual education plans, individual behaviour plans and therapy programmes. These will all need to be discussed and agreed with parents and carers so the observations need to be clearly understood by parents. For parents the language used should be free of jargon, acronyms or phrases that may be ambiguous. It is essential to use the same terminology as parents do for their child with SEN. For example, parents may not consider a child who is deaf to have a hearing impairment, but may refer to the child's Deafness instead.

Sharing observations with outside agencies and other professionals

Observations for outside agencies will need to be accurate and contain more specific details than an average observation. This may include observations linked to a therapy programme. For example, a speech and language programme may specifically be looking for evidence of a child's expressive disorder. This means practitioners must keep a very careful note of exactly what is said, how it is said and possibly when and where. Practitioners may need to be able to use and understand technical terminology to give an accurate representation of their observations. For some practitioners this may require specialist training courses, or 'on the job' training with the therapist, to ensure that terms are used in the correct context.

For some children with SEN, observations may need to record even the slightest incident. For children who are on the autistic spectrum, for example, it may not be obvious to the casual observer what has upset a child on the spectrum. It may be as simple as another child brushing against them or their toy not being in the correct place on the shelf. Therefore, the practitioner making the observations needs to understand context and have a good understanding of the individual child. In practice, this may mean that only the key person can do observations. Without the correct level of detail, multi-agency professionals will find it difficult to reach conclusions and this may affect the time taken to reach a diagnosis.

Observations to support diagnosis

Sometimes observations are required to support the suspicions of practitioners that there is a special educational need. These observations will need to be shared with parents and possibly outside agencies. They need to build up a complete picture of the child, so need to contain observations from all parts of the setting: indoors, outdoors, construction area, water and sand tables, etc. The observations may focus on one aspect of development only, for example emotional development or behavioural development. Particularly for behavioural issues, the observations may also need to record the antecedent, as well as the behaviour and consequence, known as the ABC approach (Antecedent, Behaviour, Consequence) (Riddall-Leech 2003). The antecedent is the event, which happens before the behaviour. This could be immediately before, such as an incident with another child, or some time before, such as an occurrence at home before the child comes into the setting. The practitioner may have to become a detective to try to find the common cause!

Example box

One little girl's behaviour was causing concern at her nursery. Although she was normally cheerful, popular and likable, she had started to have periods of defiance and destructive behaviour. Her key person made detailed observations, using the ABC approach, where the Antecedent, Behaviour and consequence were recorded. Her key person also noted the time when each incident occurred and how long it lasted.

When she had recorded several occurrences, the key person analysed her observations and found that all the incidents occurred about ten minutes before snack or lunchtime. Working with the theory that her child was getting hungry and this was affecting her behaviour, the key person arranged to have a drink ready ten minutes before meals or snack. This alleviated the behavioural problems almost immediately.

Assessment of the child with SEN

Assessment of children with SEN can have very different connotations. It may be used interchangeably with diagnosis and practitioners should be careful about their role in this part of the process. A diagnosis of SEN can only be made by outside agencies, unless the practitioner is trained and qualified to do so. However, practitioners can make an assessment of the child's development, as with any other child.

Standardized assessments, such as the British Picture Vocabulary Scale II (BPVS II) used by speech and language therapists (Dunn et al. 1997) for example, may be useful. These must be validated by an official organization, relevant and appropriate (Drifte 2010). Assessment may also include assessment of the effectiveness of a therapy programme. This would be making initial observations at the beginning of a programme and then comparing the child's developmental level at the end of the programme.

Planning for the child with SEN

Previously I have discussed how planning links to assessment and observations and how the child is at the centre of the process, leading and shaping the cycle.

For children with SEN the planning has to incorporate any therapy programmes and could well take the form of an individual education plan (IEP) or individual behaviour plan (IBP). This form of planning needs to be agreed with parents or carers and the multi-professional team in advance, in writing. This is usually done in a joint meeting with the parents, child (where appropriate), special educational needs coordinator (SENCO), key person and outside agency representative.

The aim is to set targets for the child to achieve. These must be SMART, i.e.:

- Specific
- Measurable
- Achievable
- Relevant
- Time bounded

In addition they must be an amalgamation of the expert specialist knowledge of the outside agency, the SEN knowledge of the SENCO and the in-depth knowledge of the key person about the child. For example, the speech and language therapist will know that the child needs more phonological awareness, the SENCO will have the resources for activities to support this and the key person will know that their key child will enjoy doing this outdoors.

Example box

Henry is a very determined, cheerful boy, with a great sense of humour. He has cerebral palsy that affects his sense of balance and movement.

The physiotherapist has given the setting a programme of exercises for Henry to do, one of which is to walk on a slope. This has been expressed in his SMART targets as:

- To walk, with support on one side only, on a slope.
- To be achieved by the next physiotherapist visit.

The SENCO has provided Henry's key person with 'wobble boards' – boards of wood with an uneven surface underneath. Henry can stand on these, with support from his key person, and rock from side to side, so he can experience the rocking motion, supporting his vestibular system.

Once he is confident with these, Henry's key person takes him to the garden outside where there is a small hill that he can practise walking up and down. After two weeks and with practice Henry can start to do this with a minimal amount of help.

When the physiotherapist visits the following month, she is very pleased with Henry's progress. She reassesses his SMART targets, asking Henry's key person to encourage him to use the steps, rather than the ramp, whenever possible.

In this example, there would be no benefit to following Henry's interest (of rolling down the hill) instead of walking. In this case, the very specific aim of walking down the hill needed to be met.

The observations will need to be explicitly linked to the targets and accurately reflect the exact outcome of the programme. It could be that some targets were met easily and well within the time frame, whereas others were more difficult. This needs to be noted so the therapist can adjust the difficulty levels accordingly.

Including therapy plans in the setting's planning

It is highly likely that the suggestions for activities and programmes that the therapist makes will be suitable for all the children in the setting. Some examples are:

- Speech and language for child with a hearing impairment: giving short, clear instructions and talking to children at eye level, so they can see your face clearly.
- A child with dyspraxia: using the exercise large ball to balance and roll on.
- Child on the autistic spectrum: a visual timetable with the daily routine displayed at children's eye level.
- Child with a visual impairment: outline the doorframe and steps with white paint or tape so it can be seen against the background easily.
- Child with challenging behaviour: strong behaviour policy, understood by all, but most importantly the children, including 'golden rules' displayed in a suitable manner, for example pictures for younger children.

> ## Example box
>
> A therapist suggests that the setting has a 'smell' and colour of the day, to support a child who is on the autistic spectrum. This will give context to his day, so he knows what to expect for the rest of the day.
>
> The SENCO decides to introduce this to the whole setting, with the hallway having a scented spray and a coloured fabric used during circle time or 'meet and greet' session. For example, Monday is orange, with an orange scented spray and an orange velvet cloth on the carpet; Tuesday is lavender, with a purple cloth, etc.
>
> Within a few weeks all the children have learned the names of the days of the week and their order.

This is very different to other planning because the outcomes are so prescriptive. The observations need to be closely linked to the targets so they can be used as evidence of progress. It is likely that, as well as written observations, the therapist will need to see the child's progress.

It may be that children already have a formal assessment from an outside agency which includes a therapy programme that the setting has to include in their planning. Very often the suggestions from a therapist can benefit all the children and including them may be good practice.

Occasionally it is necessary to have a practitioner working one to one with a child, for example on a speech and language programme. In an ideal world there would be an inclusion worker available specifically to do this. However, a lot of settings have to find time to do this in the normal course of the day. This would need to be incorporated into the everyday planning to allow this to happen.

Equally it could be that your child only needs the planning differentiated, rather than a separate set of plans. For example, allowing more time to complete an activity or breaking an activity down into smaller or more achievable steps.

Working with a multi-agency team

The observation, assessment and planning for children with SEN may need to be reviewed with the SENCO for the setting, to ensure continuity of care, especially if your child attends another setting as well, but also to oversee the effectiveness of the therapy programmes.

It can be quite daunting to have your observation, assessment and planning checked over like this, but you have to remember this is in order to support your child. The SENCO can be a great support, offering advice on how best to achieve the aims of the programme and also practical help, such as providing cover in the room when you are doing a one to one programme. Drifte (2010) suggests that part of the SENCO's role is to assess colleagues' needs, by asking them about their wants and needs first.

Monitoring observation, assessment and planning

It is the responsibility of the SENCO to monitor and track all the IEPs, IBPs, statutory assessments and therapy plans in the setting. This can be a mammoth job if there are several children with SEN, so helping your SENCO do this is important.

Monitoring a child's plans and programmes means checking they are:

- meeting the SMART targets;
- up to date at all times, to ensure each child meets their potential, and also in case the therapist should happen to need them at short notice;
- still relevant for the child. If a target has been far exceeded well before the time designated, it would be worth contacting the health professional to ask advice and set a new target;
- being recorded in enough detail and with the correct information.

Information box

It is worth getting to know your SEN policy to ensure you are meeting all the requirements. For example:

- Are you required to have observations translated into the parent's home language?
- Do you need to attend SEN meetings or will you need to brief the SENCO prior to the meeting?
- Who will liaise with the outside agencies to arrange visits and updates?
- Are there standardized formats for observations for children with SEN?

Talking to parents and carers

One of the hardest aspects of being a practitioner is approaching parents and carers when you have a concern about their child. For some parents it may be a relief to have their suspicions confirmed by someone else, but for others it may be a shock or result in denial (Drifte 2010). It is essential that you have plenty of relevant observations before you consider talking to parents, and it may be worthwhile talking your suspicions over with your colleagues.

In general, parents and carers are unlikely to understand the sort of language that is used within the childcare sector (scaffolding means a metal structure to most people!) so it is important to read over the observations and prepare any further explanatory notes. In addition, observations must be respectful and honest, so parents and carers can get an accurate picture of their child at the setting.

Unless specifically trained and qualified, practitioners cannot make a diagnosis of SEN. It is sensible to be aware of the sort of observations that the outside agencies find useful, partly to aid the process of diagnosis, if this becomes necessary, and partly so parents and carers can make their own observations at home.

Example box

Grace's key person, Rose, had noticed that sometimes she didn't follow instructions, such as getting her coat ready to go out, although most of the time she was very well behaved. Rose started to watch for the times when Grace didn't seem to be listening and made some observations of these. She also noticed that Grace always positioned herself right at the front of the group during story time.

From the observations, Rose started to see it was when Grace was absorbed in play or with her back to the practitioners that she was ignoring others. As an experiment, Rose started to turn the lights on and off at times when the children's attention was needed, such as tidy up time. Grace always responded when this was done.

Then Rose planned some musical activities, which involved listening closely to the different musical instruments. Rose made careful observations of Grace's responses. Grace seemed to struggle with some instruments, but not others.

From all these observations, Rose was beginning to suspect Grace was having problems with her hearing. Rose was able to plan suitable activities to support her suspicions, which gave her evidence to talk to the parents about.

Rose's observations were positive, focusing on how well behaved and attentive Grace normally was, but also honest, highlighting the sorts of times when Grace was struggling.

In this case the parents had also noticed that Grace seemed to have 'selective hearing', but had put it down to her age. With Rose's support, the parents were able to make their own observations, confirming that Grace was less likely to listen when she couldn't see the speaker's face or was unaware that she was being addressed.

Legislation that affects SEN

Attitudes towards children and adults with disabilities have been transformed over the last century or so. It was only as recently as 1886, with the Idiots Act, that there existed the idea that some 'idiots' could be educated and improved (Jones 1972: 185). The Mental Deficiency Act 1913 started to 'classify' the different grades of mental deficiency, from idiot, through imbecile and feeble-minded to morally defective (Jones 1972). These had very specific definitions and may seem very derogatory in today's world, including unmarried mothers being 'morally defective'.

Since then, medical knowledge has improved, social attitudes have changed enormously and there has been 'radical change to curriculum and pedagogy' (Nutbrown and Clough 2006: 39). In 1978 the Warnock report addressed these changes, with recommendations that children should be identified as 'children with learning difficulties' (Warnock 1978: 338); that there should be better assessment of special needs (p. 339); that nursery education provision should be 'substantially increased' and that play groups should accept children with disabilities (p. 343). Many of these recommendations went on to be enshrined in the 1981 Education Act, with the development of the SEN code of practice in the 1996 Education Act.

In 1995 the Disability Discrimination Act (DDA) was enacted to counter discrimination in the workplace, employment, access to goods and facilities. The 2001 Special Educational Needs and Disability Act (SENDA) increased the remit of the DDA, to ensure that schools, colleges, universities and other educational establishments did not discriminate on the grounds of disability.

This has been updated and incorporated into the Equality Act 2010, which has 'replaced previous anti-discrimination laws with a single act to make the law simpler and to remove inconsistencies' (Home Office 2012).

The 2012 Government has launched a review of SEN provision, entitled *Support and Aspiration*, which has aims to:

- ensure early identification and support of children's special educational needs;

- provide staff with knowledge, understanding and skills in order to give suitable support to their children;
- give parents information about what their local services can provide and give them greater control over the use of these services;
- arrange an integrated assessment and Health and Care Plan from birth to 25.

(DfE 2012c)

It is hoped that, by 2014, there will be a single, streamlined assessment process; that there will be a uniting Education, Health and Care Plan, bringing services together; and that families will be able to access a 'personal budget'. The changes in the last one hundred years have been significant and it is to be expected that there will be further changes in the future.

Gifted and talented

Having a child who is gifted and/or talented has some issues in common with a child who has SEN. Development and rate of development will be atypical, meaning the child will have additional needs, but these will be to stretch and challenge the child effectively. Development will be lop-sided, with more progress in the area of talent. Other areas of learning and development may be further behind their expected level for the child's age. One of the largest problems with identifying children who are gifted and talented is that children's development is so diverse in the early years that it may just be a temporary 'surge', rather than an enduring talent. It is suggested in the National Strategies document *Finding and Exploring Young Children's Fascinations* (2010: 12) that practitioners need 'to be constantly alert to each child's unique pattern of learning and development' in order to identify children who are gifted and talented.

Although the original EYFS (DfES 2008) practice guidance stated that 'there must be appropriate challenges for gifted and talented children' (p. 6), the revised EYFS (Early Education 2012) does not single out gifted and talented as a separate requirement to be addressed.

Key learning points

There are some very significant differences to the observation, assessment and planning cycle for children with SEN; namely, writing observations for a different audience (multi-agency professionals, other settings) and jointly agreeing assessments. Planning of therapy programmes will need to be incorporated into the setting's planning and can be used to enhance the current provision for all children. The monitoring is more rigorous and may also be in conjunction with others.

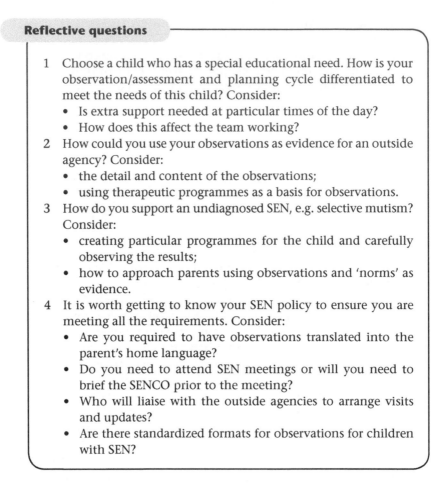

Reflective questions

1 Choose a child who has a special educational need. How is your observation/assessment and planning cycle differentiated to meet the needs of this child? Consider:
 • Is extra support needed at particular times of the day?
 • How does this affect the team working?
2 How could you use your observations as evidence for an outside agency? Consider:
 • the detail and content of the observations;
 • using therapeutic programmes as a basis for observations.
3 How do you support an undiagnosed SEN, e.g. selective mutism? Consider:
 • creating particular programmes for the child and carefully observing the results;
 • how to approach parents using observations and 'norms' as evidence.
4 It is worth getting to know your SEN policy to ensure you are meeting all the requirements. Consider:
 • Are you required to have observations translated into the parent's home language?
 • Do you need to attend SEN meetings or will you need to brief the SENCO prior to the meeting?
 • Who will liaise with the outside agencies to arrange visits and updates?
 • Are there standardized formats for observations for children with SEN?

Further reading

Kim, Y., Sugawara, A. and Kim, G. (2000) Parents' perception of and satisfaction with the eligibility assessment of their children with special needs, *Early Child Development and Care*, 160(1): 133–42.
The American authors of this paper investigate the parents' view of the assessment of their children with SEN. They draw a number of interesting conclusions, including that an activity based assessment provided more opportunities to make suggestions about the testing.
Koshy, V. and Pascal, C. (2011) Nurturing the young shoots of talent: using action research for exploration and theory building, *European Early Childhood Education Research Journal*, 19(4): 433–50.

This paper investigates a set of projects, which aimed to nurture gifted and talented children aged from four to seven years of age. It explores the role of action research as well as the elements of good practice.

Coates, D., Shimmin, A. and Thompson, W. (2009) Identifying and supporting gifted children in a nursery school (kindergarten), *Gifted Education International*, 25: 22–35.

Coates et al. suggest that Laevers' Experiential Learning Involvement Scales are an effective way of identifying gifted children. They also investigate the learning environment and how it may stimulate and challenge children.

9   The reflective practitioner

The point of establishing a reflective workforce is to benefit children.
The end result is also likely to be a more interesting, enjoyable and
personally satisfying work life for the adults in the enterprise.

(Lindon 2010: 36)

Chapter objectives

- To explore what a reflective practitioner does
- To discuss some practical examples of good reflective practice

Chapter overview

Being a good reflective practitioner is emphasized throughout the EYFS.
This is quite a new idea for early years practitioners, even though it is well
established in the primary and secondary phases. This chapter investigates the background of reflective practice, critical thinking and where
it appears in the EYFS. There are some practical ideas for practitioners to
use and discussion points which could be used by individuals as part of
their own continued professional development or used in staff meetings
to provoke questioning of practice.

Introduction

Being a reflective practitioner has a number of benefits in terms of
observation, assessment and planning. First, being reflective is likely to
improve your practice, which will benefit children. Second, reflective
practice helps support other staff. And finally, observations, assessments
and evaluations depend on critical thinking and reflection to make effective links between these areas. This is because observation, assessment
and planning are at the heart of understanding the child and getting to
know their interests, likes and developmental needs. Understanding a

child's thinking is difficult and we need to ensure that it is the best we can do, which is supported by reflection. But it needs to be more than just a theory or knowledge; it has got to be useful and translated into practice in the setting.

The aim of this chapter is to take some of the theories and translate these into accessible, practical models that can be used in any setting and we start by considering some of the influential theorists and models in this area.

Dewey

John Dewey has had influence in many areas of education, including reflective professional practice, long before it was a common idea. He was considered to be 'controversial' because, in the era when he was writing, teaching was still very formal (Gray and MacBlain 2012). His most notable books were published at the beginning of the twentieth century (*How We Think* was originally published in 1910). He is credited with developing the stages of reflective practice, from perplexity and confusion, through interpretation leading to a hypothesis (Pound 2005).

In *How We Think*, Dewey suggests that reflective practice will, by necessity, involve some 'mental unrest' as the preference to accept things at face value is resisted. The situation needs to be judged, the arguments balanced and considered. It is not always the comfortable option: 'Reflective thinking, in short, means judgment suspended during further inquiry; and suspense is likely to be somewhat painful' (p. 13).

Kolb

David Kolb constructed a theory of experiential learning (1984), which states that successful learning comes from four, sequential processes:

1   **Concrete experience** This is something you have experienced or done. This could be an activity you have done with a group of children, for example.
2   **Reflective observation** This is the reflection on the experience – how much the children enjoyed the activity or who engaged with it.
3   **Abstract conceptualization** What have you learned from this experience? Did the children learn? Why did only certain children join you?
4   **Active experimentation** This means using your new-found knowledge in real life situations. For example, based on the previous activity, you set up the table in a different way to encourage both boys and girls to join in, by using different colours, not just pinks and purples.

Schön

Donald Schön (1983) popularized the notion of reflective practice in his seminal book *The Reflective Practitioner*. He coined a number of terms, including 'reflection in action', 'reflection on action' and 'artistry'.

Reflection in action (p. 49) is when a person is critically assessing the situation or activity while it is actually happening. For example, in a setting this could be thinking about the tabletop activity where children have chosen not to engage with the activity. The game evidently holds no interest for the children in the setting at that time. A reflective practitioner will be sensitive to the fact that the children have chosen not to join the game, and will swap it for something more enjoyable. This is what Lindon (2010) refers to as 'professional thoughtfulness'.

Reflection on action (p. 276) happens after the activity or day has finished. It is looking back on the achievements, and possibly opportunities that were missed, that day.

Artistry is when an experienced and knowledgeable practitioner combines technical knowledge with intuition, experience, trial and error (Schön 1983). It is often the thing we call 'being good with children' – a difficult to describe ability combining a range of strategies, versatility and expertise, used appropriately for the situation at hand.

Schön goes on to explain about knowing in action and how this is a 'spontaneous behaviour of skilful practice' (p. 51). He uses the example of a tightrope walker and how he 'knows' what to do when walking the wire. Explaining the dynamics of how to do this is possible, but there are skills and expertise, which are very difficult, if not impossible to convey. This is termed 'tacit knowing'.

Information box

Tacit knowledge in the early years

Tacit knowledge was a term first used by Michael Polanyi in 1958 and later expanded in his book *Tacit Dimension* in 1966. It is a definition of knowledge or a process that is hard to explain to other people 'we know more than we can tell' (Polanyi 1966: 4). He uses the example of recognizing someone's face from a choice of thousands, even a million, other faces. How do we 'know' this is the right person? We could describe the eye colour, hair or shape of the nose, but the unique way these are combined together – the manner in which these make the face we recognize – is very difficult to describe.

This can be the same as pinning down those feelings and observations that you find difficult to explain when working with children. As an early years practitioner you will sometimes be doing an activity and instinctively 'know' the sorts of extension activities that the children will enjoy and engage with. This is termed 'finding the groove' by Schön (1983: 55) and he postulates that it is a form of reflection, using a combination of know-how, reflection in action *and* reflection on action. Csikszentmihalyi (2002) discusses how people who thoroughly enjoy their work – no matter what sector they work in or job they do – find that the time passes unnoticed and the person becomes totally absorbed in their activity. He termed this a 'flow experience' (p. 40) and suggests that it not only makes the job more enjoyable, but also builds self-confidence and skills.

Trying to explain tacit knowledge to another practitioner is hard, but it can be supported by reflective practice. A greater understanding of your own mastery will be achieved by reflection on (or reflection in) the things you do every day. Being able to articulate your skills is the starting point for sharing this information. This will then begin to make your tacit knowledge visible, helping you to improve your practice and share it with others.

Due to the vocational nature of the role, this is particularly pertinent for an early years practitioner. When you are with the children you are constantly using your know-how in action. Its one of the things that makes childcare so interesting, varied and exhausting!

Reflection vs observation

An observation is generally from one point of view. There is an intended outcome or audience and the observation is written with that in mind. Reflective thinking, however, must involve many points of view. It may be that the points of view contradict each other or they may be different facets of the same problem. Moon (2008) describes it as 'multiple perspectives, engagement with relevant prior experience... taking into account the broader concepts of the issues' (p. 129).

But, there are plenty of transferable skills between the two that practitioners can make use of:

- **Accuracy** You need to be accurate. For reflection this needs to be what you are actually thinking or feeling, not what you think your tutor or colleagues may want to see written. If you haven't enjoyed or understood an activity or session you must say so – or else it can't be improved.
- **Dated** It is important to keep a time line, to show progress over time and this may be significant later. For example, after a course you realize that you were beginning to understand the children more. Looking back in your diary, you realize that it was about a week after attending a course on sustained shared thinking.

There are also differences:

- You may only do reflective diary or log at certain times, for example, at the end of the course or after a piece of research. Although you should always be thinking reflectively, you may want to record reflective thoughts, as it seems appropriate.
- It should be a diagnosis, assessment and evaluation all rolled into one.
- A reflective account may contain references to literature, previous reading, magazines, etc.
- A reflective diary should be in the first person.
- It may contain 'negatives' as well as positives.
- In some cases it may be in the form of a video diary or blog.

Audience

As with observations, the reflective account should be written with an intended audience in mind. This will affect what you write and how it is written.

Professional

These may be reflective accounts for courses such as teacher training or Masters. The content should be relevant to the course and may make reference to books that have been referred to or research. They are likely to be more in-depth with full explanations. You may be given a framework for writing these sorts of accounts.

Personal

This may start as a form of mind dump while you find your own style. Once you have found a natural style for yourself, whether this is bullet points, long prose or mind map, you can start to really develop reflective thoughts. You may wish to include personal observations, links to literature or references to previous experiences.

Discussion

These may be discussion points that you wish to use in supervision or team meetings. The reflective points may be based within a framework. For example, reflection on an age range or a time of day which may not be working as well as the rest of the day.

Public

Lindon (2010: 74) recommends that reflective diaries should not be made public. However, there may be times when sharing a reflection on a public forum or blog may be useful. Having other people's viewpoint may advance knowledge and challenge thoughts. This is particularly important if you are working alone, as a childminder for example, or do not feel able to share your reflections with colleagues just yet.

In general, it is sensible to use language which is not offensive and not to make comments that condemn others. Lindon (2010) emphasizes this, saying to be wary of writing offhand remarks, which could be open to misinterpretation or just plain embarrassing (p. 55). Reflective comments should not always be about what to improve or looking at what went wrong. They must also include the things you would like to do more of, the positive experiences.

Information box

Johari's window

Part of reflective practice is having a self-awareness of your own personality, prejudices, stereotyping and viewpoint. If you are not aware of these, then your reflective practice may always be seen through only one lens.

In 1955, while researching group dynamics, Joseph Luft and Harry Ingham developed a model that purports to describe your personality, as seen by yourself and by others. They called it the Johari window – Jo (from Joseph) Hari (from Harry) – because it is represented as a four pane window frame. It consists of four areas (or rooms) which translate to four areas of your personality:

The first area is the open area – the part that you know about yourself and that others also know about, for example being dependable and friendly. The second area is the blind self – what others know about you, but which you are unaware of. For example, you may not be aware that others consider you to be mature – It's not an attribute that you would choose to describe yourself, but its something that others can see in you. The third area is the hidden self – the area that you know about yourself, but choose not to share with others. For example, you may not reveal to others that you can be tense or that you are religious.

The fourth area is the unknown self – that area of your personality of which both you and others are unaware. For example, you may not be able to predict how you would react to an emergency situation. Would you be calm and in control? Or would you panic?

This knowledge can throw a light on how you work or interact with children or with colleagues. For example, in your reflective diary you may notice that you often come up with unusual ideas for activities that no one else in the room had considered. In this case you are unaware that you are ingenious. Once identified, this can be used to your advantage to help support others with new ideas or you may wish to start a folder of good ideas for everyone to use.

Completing the Johari window

To determine your personality traits you have to choose from a list of 56 adjectives which best describe yourself. Your friends and/or colleagues then do the same. The overlapping traits (known areas) and differences (unknown areas) can then be compared. You can do this yourself on line at: http://kevan.org/johari

Methods of recording reflections and reflective practice

There are likely to be as many methods of reflection as there are practitioners. Each person will keep their reflective accounts in a different way. Some ideas are suggested here, but you may prefer a mixture of these, depending on the circumstances, or have a totally unique way of recording your reflections. The important things are that it is effective for you, is easily integrated into your work and is used to inform subsequent practice.

Daily diary

The practitioners carry these throughout the day, so that thoughts and ideas can be jotted down immediately. This may include reflection on individual activities, room management or interactions between children. This is an example of 'reflection in action' as defined by Schön.

Room diary or log

This is kept in the room and it is used as a central base for all practitioners to keep notes on the day's activities. This may sometimes be 'reflection in action' while it is happening or 'reflection on action' afterwards. These can then be used in staff meetings or room meetings to bring together common themes or to discuss differences. This is a great way to recognize good practice and help embed it into the setting.

Personal diary or journal

This may be a very personal diary, just for you to record your emotions, inner thoughts and misgivings. You may not wish to share this with anyone, but use it for your own reflections. Sometimes it can be cathartic just to write the issues down and review them dispassionately at a later date.

Mind maps

Tony Buzan (Buzan and Buzan 1995) popularized mind mapping, which is a similar technique to spidergrams or concept maps. The initial activity or experience is written in a central point on the paper. Reflective thoughts are written on lines coming from the centre, one thought per line. Colours are useful to differentiate between the different lines of thought. Each reflection is developed in finer detail as it moves away from the centre, until there are a number of detailed analyses around the circumference of the diagram. This is a good method for visual learners and can be very quick because only keywords or phrases are used.

Mood boards or drawings

Visual learners may also prefer to draw their reflections, or use images from magazines or the internet. Brief notes accompanying the illustrations describe the reflection and can be used to explain the relevance of the images to other practitioners. Garvey and Lancaster (2010) suggest this could be approached in the same way as a mind map, with a central illustration 'as long as you know what our squiggles, arrows, dots and lines mean' (p. 30).

Voice recording

It may be more convenient to voice-record reflective thoughts, maybe at the end of the day when travelling home. Many mobile phones now have record capabilities and this is a good method for auditory learners to use.

Recording your reflections, whichever method is used, will take some time, but it is likely to get faster as you find a style that suits you. It could be argued that it will save time in the future because it will reduce mistakes, identify areas for personal development and make your role more effective. This is also known as 'praxis' (see information box).

When Harkin (2005) investigated how professionals in the higher education sector engaged with reflective practice, he found that, after the initial training period was completed, it was very difficult for teachers to maintain their reflective processes. Harkin goes on to propose that reflective practice needs to be part of the 'institutional conditions' (p. 176) to be effective and long lasting.

Information box

Praxis

Praxis is about using the theories of reflective practice in your daily work with children. One way to think about this is as the final quadrant in the circle, completing the cycle of reflection:

1 doing the activity or having the experience;
2 reflecting on this, using your choice of reflective method;
3 linking your reflections to theory, EYFS, child development, etc., making sense of the reflections;
4 praxis – reinvesting the links, theory and reflections back into your practice with the children.

In many respects praxis is the most important part of the process because reflection, without going back to use it in practice, is just an academic exercise. Appleby (2010) suggests that praxis is the internalization of the reflective journey 'involving personal and professional qualities and attributes that merge as the individual assumes ownership ... and develops a personal sense of responsibility for the outcomes for children' (p. 9).

Whalley (2007) discusses praxis in terms of sharing a dialogue with parents and how observations and reflections by staff supported their work with parents. She defines praxis as 'learning by doing, and then spending time thinking about what you have done and making links between theory and practice' (p. 122).

Critical thinking

Appleby (2010) teases out the importance of a critical stance when being reflective. She discusses how reflection should not be 'mechanistic' (p. 9) but must be suitable for the individual practitioner or group of practitioners. Practising being reflective and ensuring there is a safe emotional environment for practitioners can achieve this. As a practitioner a 'critical' friend can be vital, where critical means 'expressing an analysis of the merits' (a dictionary definition). Your critical friend can offer support but must also be able to challenge your thinking, to enable your thinking to move on. There may be occasions where your critical friend may play 'devil's advocate', taking an opposing viewpoint to encourage further discussion. Paige-Smith and Craft (2007) endorse having a critical friend, to 'bounce our ideas off . . . and to co-construct understandings and ideas' (p. 22). Moon (2008) further suggests this should be a reciprocal role. This may take the form of practitioner peer observations, where practitioners observe each other in the setting and then feedback their observations. This is beneficial for both observer and observed. It is sensible to have some training on observing adults and giving feedback if practitioners are new to this, to get the most from the process.

Links to the EYFS

The EYFS (DfE 2012b) has reflection embedded in the Statutory Framework for planning and assessment. When talking about planning children's activities, it states that practitioners *must* 'reflect on the different ways that children learn and reflect these in their practice'. Similarly, the Statutory Framework demands that practitioners observe children and 'then shape learning experiences for each child reflecting those observations' (DfE 2012b: 10). This not only requires knowledge of child development and planning, but also the skills to reflect upon these and use appropriate methods to put them into practice.

Similarly in the guidance document, Development Matters (Early Education 2012), practitioners are asked to reflect on guidance in columns headed 'Positive Relationships' and 'Enabling Environments' (p. 3) to inform their own practice. In addition, it is good practice to have reflection with parents on their child's progress (p. 10) and to support children with their reflective skills (p. 11 and p. 18).

The challenges of reflective practice

As with anything new there may be challenges to be overcome. The biggest challenge that many practitioners new to reflective practice initially face is finding time to write their diaries or record their thoughts. This is partly because the habit has not yet been formed and partly because there is usually a hesitation from practitioners to record their innermost thoughts. However, as confidence grows and the benefits start to become apparent, time may not be considered an issue any more.

Before practitioners embark on reflective practice it is sensible to have a staff meeting or training course, so everyone is aware of the expectations and methods available. Reflection done well takes expertise, skill and practice.

It is worth mentioning here that sometimes reflection can be an emotional experience. You may have to consider whether you are emotionally able to cope with self-reflection, particularly if you are looking back on a negative experience. Of course, it may also be a very self-affirming process if you are reflecting on a positive experience.

Key learning points

This chapter has considered the role of reflective practice as a necessary skill for professionals working in the early years. Although some of the theories are generic – Schön considered a range of job roles and Dewey investigated many areas of education – they still echo good practice in the early years. The discussion of the links and differences between observation and reflective practice show that there are many similarities.

Using reflective practice in your setting should be an underlying theme in everything you do, including observation, assessment, planning, evaluation, CPD and working with parents. The method you use should suit your personal requirements, and may change over time. There are some challenges, such as time and being emotionally secure, but these have to be addressed so you can fulfil your role as a fully rounded practitioner.

Reflective questions

1 Do you have room discussions and reflections in your room? Consider:
   - What opportunities are there?
   - What challenges are there?
   - How does the age range/gender mix/personality mix affect the room ambiance?
2 Have a room or group discussion about the sorts of reflection methods you prefer, or would like to have a go at. Consider:
   - Why would these be beneficial for you?
   - What would you hope to gain?
   - Do any of the practitioners have previous experience they could share?
3 Get down on the floor and look at the environment from a 2-year-old's perspective or use a mirror to look at the room.
   - What is appealing?
   - What is offputting?
   - What can you NOT see from the floor?

Further reading

Dyer, M. and Taylor, S. (2012) Supporting professional identity in undergraduate Early Years students through reflective practice, *Reflective
Practice*, 13(4): 551–63.
This is an interesting study focussing on how learners on early years
degrees evaluate their own performance, particularly self-reflection and
how they judge themselves. Dyer and Taylor found the learners still relied
on others to give judgements on their performance, despite being taught
about reflective practice and being confident about their own abilities.
Reed, M. and Canning, N. (eds) (2010) *Reflective Practice in the Early Years*.
London: Sage.
Reflective Practice in the Early Years has 13 chapters, each written by a different author. The chapters have been arranged to coincide with the four
EYFS themes and contain a range of viewpoints, from play to safeguarding to defining quality in the early years.

10 Observation, assessment and planning in research

Observation methods are powerful tools for gaining insight into situations

(Cohen et al. 2007: 412)

Chapter objectives

- To compare and contrast observations made during research
- To bring together reflective practice and critical observation

Chapter overview

Many courses, such as a foundation degree or degree in childhood studies, call for a piece of research in the form of a dissertation or a piece of independent study. This may be the first time that you have had to do such a piece of work. This chapter compares and contrasts the similarities and differences when observing for research rather than as part of the observation, assessment and planning cycle. Observations for research are used for a different type of assessment and will not be used for planning in the setting, but usually to gather data to answer questions, test a theory or formulate a theory. It could be that your observations create a question, or that a question is already in your mind to be answered by the observations.

Observations for research

There are many similarities between observing children for research and for assessment and planning needs. However there are some significant differences as well, which experienced practitioners can find very frustrating because they expect the two situations to be the same.

Similarities

The observations have to be accurate, reliable, valid and honest. A variety of different observation methods will still be applicable and these will be selected according to the data that needs to be gathered, just as observations are made for assessment and planning.

In both cases there will have to be a conclusion or an analysis of the observations. In research analysis all the observations should be considered through different lenses, and different points of view should be considered. This is useful for observations for assessment, but not essential as it is for research. The outcome of the observations may not be predictable: although this is not critical for observations used for assessment, for research this may be the very thing that makes the subject interesting to record. For example, would replacing all the toys in the home corner with pink toys dissuade the boys from playing there?

Account must still be made of reactivity because children may still react to being observed, whatever the reason for doing the observation, which must be taken into account as to how this may affect the research results.

Differences

Ethics

Ethics were briefly mentioned in Chapter 2, in terms of being respectful when observing children. When observing children for research, you may have to submit your ideas to an ethics committee for approval before you can even start your observations. It is to ensure that the safety and rights of children are paramount in everything that you do. If you do start observations before the research has been approved, these may not be used in your final dissertation or study. This is not foolproof, however. Powell and Smith (2006) found that, in New Zealand, there was more emphasis on the ethics of the initial consent from children than on their continued protection throughout the research study. Schrag (2011) argues that 'better options exist' (p. 120) than ethics committees.

Anonymity

When doing observations for assessment it is essential that the child or children can be identified, but the observations in research may need to be anonymous (Mukherji and Albon 2010). This means that when you are making notes of your observations, either in the setting or afterwards, you will need to have a robust way of linking the child with their pseudonym. If when you come to write up the observations you are no longer sure who 'Child A' is, this could be very confusing and make the observations worthless.

Method

For observations for assessment in your own setting you will not need to ask for permission. Most settings request parents' and carers' permission to make these observations as part of the daily routine. However, for research you must obtain separate written permission and negotiate times that you can do observations (Cohen et al. 2007).

The type of observation you will do for research will be determined by the research methodology. Sometimes the observation may be on a specific area of learning development, such as speech and language, or the observations may be very general if the theory is being developed, as you may do with grounded theory. The manner of the research will decide in advance whether you are a participant or a non-participant in the children's play. Under normal circumstances you would be able to put aside your observation at any time to go and join in with the children's play. However, when doing research this would jeopardize the data collection, so you must be very conscious at all times of your own actions and reactions.

Information box

Continuum of participation in observations

Whether you are a participant or not in the children's play is not something that you would normally consider. However, for research this may make a critical difference to the outcome, because your actions (or, indeed lack of them) may affect how the child or children react to a situation.

The amount of participation will lie somewhere on the following continuum:

Full participation You, as the observer, fully participate in the group, without telling the group that you are doing research. Mukherji and Albon (2010) suggest that this is unethical, because there is no opportunity for members of the group to opt out. This would be equivalent to not telling the children that you are doing some research for college or not allowing them the opportunity to walk away from the activity.

Participant as observer You would be a full member of the group, but everyone is aware of the research, have given consent and are able to withdraw from the research at any time. You will be involved with many aspects of the setting and may use several different observational methods. This is one of the most common methods when doing research in your own setting or when you are doing action research.

Observer as participant You will spend some time with the group and may be only observing one area of activity or setting routine, such as outdoor play or children arriving. The participants are fully aware of the research, have given consent and may withdraw from the research at any time. You may be an observer as participant if you are doing a baby room placement, for example.

Complete observer You would not be involved with the group at all, for example observing children in a public place or watching babies through the baby room window, without interacting at all. This method raises questions about ethics as well. Can informed consent be given if the participants are not aware that they are part of a research study? Should parents and carers be asked?

(adapted from Mukherji and Albon 2010: 107)

The advice to observe children everywhere and at all times may not be relevant when doing your research. The research will determine when and where you will do your observations. It could be that this will be a specific place or time of day and may be critical to the outcomes of the research. For example, if your research is around attachment and how parents and carers experience the handover procedure at the setting, it is essential that you see the handover procedure. This may be something that you have to practise first, if you don't already observe at this time of day. Similarly, you may not have to observe every child, but it may be a focus group or focus child.

Example box

For my research I observed children in mixed age groups. When recording observations I had to ensure that the age difference between the children was greater than 12 months, because in my methodology I had defined mixed age groups as being groups of children where the age difference was greater than 12 months.

Any examples of interactions that were not mixed age had to be disregarded.

Tick sheets are not normally encouraged as a method of observation, because they do not give the detail or context that a written observation does. However, for research this may be an ideal way of recording many observations of children, which would not be physically possible by writing everything longhand.

Writing up observations

When writing up observations the context needs to be recorded, for example socio-economic situation or cultural background (Roberts-Holmes 2005: 96). This would not normally be of importance when writing up observations for assessment, because each child is being considered as an individual, not as a product of their background or family. It is irrelevant, for example, that a child has poor physical development because there is no opportunity to play outside at home. It is the practitioner's role to support the physical development while at the setting. However, for the research it could be vitally important to record that the setting is the only place where that child has the opportunity to play outside.

The language that is used in writing up observations for research will be very different from the language you would normally use. For example, the research may include reference to different types of views, such as feminist discourse or gender and discourse.

Time

Making observations in the setting should fit in with the daily routine and not reduce the amount of time spent with the children. This may be achieved when doing research by using methods such as video recording or audio recording, but in general observations for research will take longer. The other advantage of recording observations for research is that they can be re-watched or listened to again and again (Mukherji and Albon 2010) to ensure nothing has been missed.

Differences in assessment

Most observations have some value when assessing them for planning. However, when considering observations for research, it may be that some are irrelevant perhaps because they fall outside the focus group or are used purely for quantitative methods.

Information box

The difference between qualitative and quantitative assessment

As part of your research project you will come across two expressions – qualitative and quantitative.

Quantitative data, with a word root of 'quantity', concerns numerical data and is usually linked to the reliability of data. For example, this may be the number of times that a child visits the painting table, or how many boys play with girls.

Qualitative data, with a word root of 'quality', concerns the quality, details or descriptive nature of the data. For example, does a child visit the painting table voluntarily or are they called over to paint? Or, do the boys approach the girls to play or is it vice versa? Cohen et al. (2007) differentiate between the two types as the observation of facts 'such as the number of books in a classroom' and behaviours, for example the 'friendliness of the teacher' (p. 396).

Mukherji and Albon define quantitative observations as giving 'standardised, numerical data' (2010: 106) gathered from observational methods such as tracking or sociograms. On the other hand, qualitative observations are usually for 'exploratory purposes . . . usually undertaken in naturalistic situations' (p. 107) and are gathered from observational methods such as magic moments or narrative.

In research, it is important to decide on the type of observations that you will be doing in advance and to detail the methods that will be used to gather the data. This ensures that the correct type of data is collected for analysis. It could be that you will choose to use both qualitative and quantitative observations, in which case both methods should be considered and designed as part of the research plan.

More often than not, one or two observations will be enough to determine the next steps for that child. With research you will need to find more than a single next step so may need several different types of observation. It may be that you are looking for the differences in the normal, or similarities, so it could be a group of children rather than an individual child. For example, when looking at social behaviour you may need to observe several groups of children.

If you need to triangulate the data, you may need to do more than just observations; for example you may need to interview parents and hold focus groups as well.

Differences in next steps

The biggest difference with research is that there may not necessarily be a clearly defined next step. It could be that the results are not about an individual child at all, but are generalizations about children's learning. The presentation of the conclusions may also be very different. The language is likely to be academic, with links to research and published literature. The observations as individual entities may not be seen at all, if for example they have been reduced to quantitative data for graphs and tables.

The rationale for doing observations for research is different to that for observations for assessment and planning. Research should alter or inform the body of knowledge about children, early childhood education or the children's interactions. Due to the time that it takes to do research and reach the conclusions, it could be that the children involved in the research may not benefit, but it will be for the benefit of children coming afterwards. It could be that a clearly defined next step is never identified, or maybe several different recommendations are made for further research. The recommendations may be purely theoretical, never to be acted on at all.

How observations in research can support everyday observations

Observations in research should be more 'critical' (Roberts-Holmes 2005: 93) than other observations. This means that they are more reflective and dig deeper to expose the underlying causes and realities – they make the 'familiar strange' (Clough and Nutbrown 2007: 48).

Information box

Making the familiar strange

Have you ever had the feeling that things are different, but the same? This can sometimes happen if you are visiting a town you know well, only to discover a building has disappeared to be replaced by something else. Suddenly everything looks strange and different around that area. You may notice things about the other buildings that you hadn't spotted before. It could be that the area looks larger or smaller than it did before. The replacement building looks alien and out of place.

Clough and Nutbrown (2007: 48) use the analogy of travelling abroad and noticing that how people dress, the traffic systems, shopping and eating are all familiar yet different. They have termed this 'making the famil-iar strange'. So how does this relate to making observations?

It could be that you've worked in the same setting, with the same col-leagues, for many years – it may even be your own home if you are a child-minder. But have you truly, critically observed the environment, the routine, the children?

By making critical observations you may start to notice new aspects of your work. It could be that a trip to see another country's pedagogy, such as forest schools, makes you review your own outdoor area. Or it may be that a visit to a much larger setting than your own makes you appreciate the homeliness of your setting. Seeing different pedagogies enables us to reflect on our own practice, our assumptions and ourselves.

My personal experience of seeing things through a 'new and different lens' (Clough and Nutbrown 2007: 49) was reading Chris Athey's book, *Extending Thought in Young Children*, where she describes schema and schematic play in children. This was the first time I had read about schema in depth and it changed my observations of children forever. After reading it, I began to spot connections between children's play, drawings and interests. Once a schema seemed to emerge I could concentrate my observations on supporting and developing these. Familiar play suddenly became part of a pattern, some-thing larger – it started to look different through the lens of schema.

Challenges

When doing observations as part of your day-to-day work colleagues and other practitioners understand that you are observing the children. When doing observations for research however, there may be other prac-titioners who become concerned that you are observing their practice as well. You should be aware of this and make sure that they understand the limits and scope of your research.

Deciding on your degree of participation (as described earlier) can be a critical challenge for research. If you decide at the beginning to be a participant as observer (taking part in the children's play, for example) you may find that your comments and actions change the direction of the play. It is then too late to be a complete observer, so you would need to start the process again.

Documenting observations for research is very different to making daily observations. The observations will need to be categorized into the areas being researched, instead of the areas of learning and development from the EYFS. They may need to be reduced to a numeric count for quantitative data.

Depending on the type of research, it is likely that you will need to collect a large number of observations, some of which may become irrelevant as the research progresses. For example, if the original research concerned gendered play, but was then redefined as gendered play in the outdoors, the indoor observations become background material or are obsolete.

Video or audio recording observations aims to ensure that nothing is missed. However, it also produces an enormous amount of data, which has to be transcribed. This can take a massive amount of time and can be very mundane work.

Key learning points

When making observations for research there is a need to record a range of contextual data as well, the exact nature of which will depend on the question that is being researched. Before starting observations there are some essentials to consider, such as ethics and consent, and during the research the practitioner must be aware of their own involvement with the children. Although practitioners observe children all the time, there are a number of differences when observing for research that may make it a more challenging endeavour.

Reflective questions

1. If you are making observations in your own setting and you see a situation where one child is fighting with another, you would intervene in accordance with the setting's behaviour policy. Consider:
   - If you are making observations for research in someone else's room or a different setting, what would you do?
   - How would you react if you witnessed another practitioner talk harshly to a child?
2. How would you record an observation of a child playing with the building blocks as a quantitative observation and as a qualitative observation? Consider:
   - the number of blocks in each tower built;
   - the language used (colour, size, imaginative play);
   - motor skills demonstrated.

Further reading

Papatheodorou, T., Luff, P. and Gill, J. (2011) *Child Observation for Learning and Research.* Harlow: Pearson Education Ltd.
This is an in-depth book that will take you right from the beginnings of any research project, with an introduction to theorists, to the very end with different writing methods.
Solvason, C. (2012) Research and the early years practitioner-researcher, *Early Years: An International Journal of Research and Development:* 1–10. http://www.tandfonline.com/doi/full/10.1080/09575146.2012.665360 (accessed 18 November 2012).
In this paper Carla Solvason 'challenges the approach that we traditionally take to research (in the realm of Early Childhood)'. She queries the methods and language used and takes a critical view of attitudes around research, suggesting there may be better ways for the future. It is a thought-provoking view for lecturers and students alike.

11 Bringing it all together

*The educator must, simultaneously, plan ahead whilst also recognising
the significance of the here and now in a child's progress.*

(Broadhead 2006: 201)

Chapter objectives

- To bring together the observation, assessment and planning cycle
- To show – through worked examples – how the cycle comes together in
  practice

Chapter overview

In this book we have discussed each element of the observation, assessment and planning cycle, looked at how these link together and considered how a robust system can benefit children, families and practitioners.
This chapter is all about the bigger picture, bringing it all together, and
demonstrates – through a series of case studies – how observation, assessment and planning can be used simply, efficiently and successfully to
support all areas of children's learning and development. The examples
used are small vignettes, to illustrate the point being made.

Case study 1: the baby room

Carrie is 10 months old and attends the baby room for two full days a
week.

Observations

Narrative:
At lunchtime Carrie puts her fingers in the yoghurt and squeezes. She
then rubs her hands on the table, leaving a trail of sticky, squidgy yoghurt.

Delightedly, she starts to rub the yoghurt on the table, with great concentration. She spends around five minutes swirling the yoghurt round with both hands.

Magic moment:
Carrie was fascinated when I tipped water over her hands in the water tray. She kept looking at me and gurgling, wanting me to repeat it.

Tracking:
Carrie has played with the sand in the sand tray, dried pasta, the fluffy material in the book corner and has put her hands on the cold window by the back door.

Assessment

Carrie has started to feel things with her fingers, as well as putting things to her mouth (mouthing). She is beginning to understand different textures and tactile experiences. She is able to enjoy a range of sensory experiences through the continuous provision (sand, water, book corner) and has also found some additional activities (yoghurt at lunchtime).

Next steps

Category 1: child development
Carrie is within the normal parameters for physical development (8–20 months: enjoys sensory experience of making marks in damp sand, paste or paint; Early Education 2012: 22). The next step from Development Matters (Early Education 2012) is to 'make connections between their movements and marks they make' (p. 23). This could be the practitioner drawing Carrie's attention to her yoghurt 'creation' or setting up a finger painting activity so Carrie has a picture creation to look at.

This also links to the area of learning and development 'expressive arts and design' (Early Education 2012: 43). To extend this, Carrie could be allowed to crawl through the paint on a large sheet of paper, so she can see that all her body can leave marks, not just her fingers.

Category 2: extend an interest
Carrie has discovered that her fingers have a sensory feedback. This could be extended to support her proprioception (knowing where your body is in space) by attaching jingle bells wristbands onto her wrists, so they jingle when she moves. This will support her interest in the cause and effect when she moves her body.

Category 3: embed a learning point
Embedding learning is particularly important for very young children and activities should be repeated regularly so babies have the opportunity

to reinforce their learning. The next step would be more messy play, such as gloop and wet sand.

Category 4: personal, social and emotional development
Supporting Carrie's exploration of her senses is vital. Telling her she is 'naughty' for spreading yoghurt on the table will only discourage her from exploring in this way. She is far too young to understand the difference between sitting at the table playing with gloop and sitting at the table playing with her yoghurt. She should be encouraged to access all the sensory areas, and her key person should support this by showing excitement and enjoyment alongside Carrie's play.

Planning

From the next steps there are several planning outcomes:

- more messy play activities such as gloop and paint;
- gross motor skill play such as a sheet of large paper on the floor covered with paint;
- music and movement sessions where jingle bells are attached to the wrists and ankles;
- time with Carrie's key person to encourage and develop these new skills.

Case study 2: the toddler room

Jake is 30 months old and attends the toddler room five mornings a week. He is active and inquisitive and enjoys coming to nursery.

Observations

Narrative:
Jake always plays with the cars and lorries first thing in the morning. This morning his play consisted of moving them from one area of the carpet to the other, watching closely and making the appropriate noises. He encouraged his friends to 'come and play cars' and directed them to where each vehicle should be going, what the lorries were carrying and who was in the cars. When one of his friends suggested playing somewhere else, Jake suggested going outside with the small shopping cart and filling it with the beanbags there. The two boys then pushed the cart to the grass and deposited the beanbags in a heap. Jake said, 'What else can we get?' and started looking for other toys that would fit into the cart.

Magic moment:
Jake was dressed in the pink tutu, complete with matching handbag. He was very careful to choose a bag that matched his outfit and then filled the bag with his favourite cars.

Jake helped get the glue pots and brushes from the shelf, ready for our gluing activity.

Jake was playing with the dumper truck in the sand, digging and carrying sand from one end of the tray to the other.

Sociogram:
 9:00 Jake was playing with Adil, Harry and Sam on the carpet.
 9:20 Jake and Harry went outside.
 9:30 Jake and Harry were joined by Callum and Charlie.
 9:40 Jake invited Angus to join in with them.
10:30 Jake was playing by himself in the dressing up area.
10:40 Jake was with his key person, putting out the glue pots.
10:50 Jake and Mia were painting side by side. Jake was talking to Mia about who was in the train he had painted.

Assessment

Jake has a wide range of friends, who he plays with equally. He enjoys being with both children and adults, especially when he is able to help.

He will try things out (such as putting different items in his shopping cart) and problem solving (choosing the right size object for the bag).

There are some signs of a transporting schema – cars travelling, transporting in cart, digger in the sand, handbags.

Next steps

Category 1: child development
Jake has an interest in transporting objects, so encouraging his positional language (in, on, under, on top of) would be of interest to him (Early Education 2012, Mathematics p. 36). His key person could also use Jake's interest as a way to introduce shape: 'could you get me the square basket/ all the round bean bags/triangle blocks'.

Category 2: extend an interest
To explore the transporting schema, practitioners can provide resources such as large bags, small bags, baskets for the bikes outdoors, buckets and spades for the sand outdoors, scoops and containers for the water tray.

Category 3: embed a learning point
Ensure cars and trucks are out in the morning so Jake can play with them straight away. This not only embeds learning but also gives Jake an enjoyable experience when he first comes into the setting.

Category 4: personal, social and emotional development
Jake has good social development and is evidently well liked by his peers.
He is building a mastery disposition that should be encouraged and
extended, for example, by giving him more complex tasks such as finding all the triangles in the block box and bringing them to the carpet. He
appears to choose to play with other boys. This should be further investigated to see if he excludes playing with girls or not.

Planning

The planning outcomes from the next steps are:

- Continuous provision should be enhanced to include resources
  suitable for a transporting schema.
- Practitioners in the room should be made aware that Jake's positional language is being supported and extended, and that the box
  of cars needs to be out in the morning.
- More observations need to be made by Jake's key person to investigate the gender of Jake's social circle.

Case study 3: the pre-school room

Maryam is 50 months old and attends her local preschool five days a
week. She is quiet but enjoys playing with her best friend Rachel, especially with the big wooden construction blocks.

Observations

Narrative:
Maryam and Rachel were playing in the construction area. They had constructed an enclosure and were discussing where the door should be:

> Maryam: It should be near there, so it's easy to get the dinosaurs
> Rachel: But we need to get outdoors as well, so it should be here
> Maryam: Alright. (thinks for a minute) We can have two doors.
> Rachel: OK. You get the dinosaurs and I'll make the doors.

Narrative:
At circle time, we were discussing the day's play. Maryam was describing
their dinosaur enclosure.

> Maryam: We made a dinosaur zoo.
> Me: Why dinosaurs?
> Maryam: because I like dinosaurs, especially Tyrannosaurus.

Me: How did you stop them escaping?
Maryam: By making the walls really big.
Me: Were the walls really high, so they couldn't climb over?
Maryam: Yes.
Me: How else could you stop them getting out?
Maryam: (thinks for a minute) Hmmm. Put a roof on, like a cage?
Me: Yes! That would stop them getting out.
Maryam: But it would have to be strong, cos Tyrannosaurus has big, big teeth.
Me: Has he?
Maryam: Oh, yes. I saw it at the museum.
Me: Sounds fun! What else did you see?
Maryam: Triceratops and Stegosaurus. They were very big too.

Assessment

Maryam has a good knowledge of dinosaurs (they are big, strong, have big teeth and can name some). She has seen the fossils and can equate these to once being real animals. She has a limited social circle, playing almost exclusively with Rachel.

Next steps

Category 1: child development
Maryam is happy talking about the things she has seen and experienced. She should be encouraged and supported by recording her experiences and providing her with opportunities to share with the group (Early Education 2012: 40).

Her mathematical language could be extended by her key person using terms such as high, short, long, longer (Early Education 2012: 36).

Category 2: extend an interest
Dinosaurs are an obvious interest. Further observations and sustained shared thinking could elicit whether the interest is due to their size (extend by introducing other large animals such as elephants and whales) or the trip to the museum (extend by finding out what other fossils or dinosaurs Maryam saw) or the scariness of the dinosaurs (extend by introducing other animals with big teeth – sharks and lions). It could be that all these aspects interest Maryam.

Category 3: embed a learning point
Providing model dinosaurs, books on dinosaurs or a further trip to the museum would help embed this knowledge. Discussions with peers and discussions during circle time would help embed and extend Maryam's interest.

Category 4: personal, social and emotional development
Currently Maryam has a small social circle. Her interest in dinosaurs is a good springboard from which to encourage her play with like-minded children. This needs to be handled sensitively by her key person and should include Rachel as well.

Planning

The following planning outcomes are possible from these next steps:

- The home corner, or role-play area, could be turned into a dinosaur themed area, such as a volcano home or Jurassic forest, with the children helping to decide which dinosaurs lived in there.
- The children could design a 'large animal zoo' containing dinosaurs, elephants, whales, etc.
- A trip to the museum for the whole preschool, providing an opportunity for Maryam to be a 'guide' for the other children, to expand her social contacts within preschool.

Case study 4:   child with special educational needs

Derek is a quiet, shy boy, aged 35 months, who goes to a childminder three days a week. He has severe hearing loss and wears hearing aids all the time. He enjoys being with the other two children, a baby and an older girl, Alice.

Observations

Focus child – Derek, outdoors in the garden
Derek is always busy in the garden, digging in the soil, planting orange or apple pips after snack time, looking for minibeasts under the stones and sitting in the sand pit. Today he was particularly fascinated by a spider's web on the shed door and spent a long time looking at the pattern and pieces of fluff trapped in it. He then went to look at the apple tree. When I asked what he was looking at, he said 'to see if the apples are red'. He did not appear to notice the blackbird singing in the tree, but did turn round when the dog next door barked. He did not want to play football with Alice or run to the fence to look at the dog. Once at an activity he seemed happy to stay there for some time and not move.

ABC
I had noticed that Derek sometimes did not want to get his coat on to go out to play and that he was getting upset when I had to remind him.

Antecedent:
In the play room, zipping up Alice's coat. Asked Derek to get his coat.

Behaviour:
Derek ignored me and carried on playing with the cars.

Consequence:
I went over to Derek and asked him again to get his coat. He was upset at leaving his cars, but did get his coat.

Antecedent:
As I was clearing up the books, I asked Derek to get his coat.

Behaviour:
He came over and picked up a book, sat down and started to look at it.

Consequence:
I asked Derek to put the book away and get his coat. Derek gave me the book and went for his coat.

For speech and language therapist
Derek seems to be missing the beginning of words ('poon for spoon, 'og for dog, 'ark for park). Sometimes he is difficult to understand, especially if he is excited about something.

Assessment

Derek prefers to sit at something that interests him rather than moving or running around outside. This could be to do with his sense of balance and not being confident to run on an uneven lawn.

From analysing a number of the ABC observations, it became obvious that Derek was not 'cued in' or paying attention when being asked to get his coat. He only 'ignored' the childminder when she was doing something else at the same time. This could be because he wasn't aware that he was being spoken to, or that he couldn't see the childminder's face, to lip read, when she was busy elsewhere.

Next steps

Category 1: child development
Derek needs to be encouraged to improve his physical development. Although he is able to walk, run, hop, etc. (Early Education 2012: 24) he needs to have the confidence to do so. The next steps could be to encourage different forms of movement while holding the childminder's hand, and then gradually remove the support when he is more confident. Activities such as obstacle courses, even very easy ones such as walking along a wiggly rope on the floor, would support this.

The speech and language therapist gave the childminder a programme to support his speech sounds. This included a lotto game, where the pictures had to be matched. The words had the same rime (the sound the end of the word makes) but a different onset (the sound the beginning of the word makes). For example, Log and Dog, Spoon and Moon, Dark and Park. This encourages Derek to listen carefully to the beginning of the word and to differentiate between similar sounding words. The speech and language therapist also suggested that the childminder should draw Derek's attention to environmental sounds, such as the blackbird, so he is more aware of the range of sounds around him.

Category 2: extend an interest
Derek has a great interest in nature, which is supported well in the setting that he attends. Visiting different environments such as the beach and woodland, where Derek can experience different aspects of nature, different minibeasts and different sounds, can extend his interest in nature.

Category 3: embed a learning point
Derek was fascinated by the spider's web, the patterns and stickiness of it. Reading books such as Eric Carle's *Very Busy Spider* and making spider web pictures using PVA glue and sticking fluff to it, could support Derek's fascination with the web.

Category 4: personal, social and emotional development
Using Derek's name and getting his attention before talking to him will encourage him to attend and listen, as well as picking up lip reading and visual clues. This will support his personal and emotional development, because he will be more confident that he is doing what is required, rather than being confused about the instructions.

Planning

From these next steps the planning could be:

- Alice and Derek could use the word game, together with the childminder, as an activity each morning;
- a trip to the beach or woodland area;
- reading and exploring Eric Carle books and nature books;
- simple obstacle courses, getting more complex as Derek gains confidence.

Bringing it all together

In this book I have outlined a practical and usable system that ensures observations, assessments and evaluations, next steps and planning are a seamless cycle. Whether the observations are for the daily planning, a multi-agency team or for your own research, this approach puts the child at the centre of everything you do and ensures that their development is supported and nurtured effectively.

To get the greatest benefits, these techniques need to be practised and incorporated into daily life at the setting. Once you have started to observe children, ensure that your observations and assessments have meaningful next steps. Monitor and track the next steps as the child develops and make certain that these links are clear. Once embedded, these techniques will become powerful tools to ensure that your children are stretched, challenged and enjoy their time with you. The more you practise them, the more they will become second nature and part of your daily life.

The future

Since the early 2000s the early years sector has changed almost beyond recognition. In that time we have seen research showing how young children benefit by having well qualified, motivated practitioners, and the discourse about professionalism in the early years has expanded (Sylva et al. 2004; Woodrow 2008; Simpson 2010; Harwood et al. 2012; Ingelby and Hedges 2012). The EYFS has been introduced, and revised, with supporters and some opposition. Following the Tickell Review (2011), the Statutory EYFS documentation was reduced by almost a half. In the future this may be slimmed down even further, supported by the ambition to have a knowledgeable, confident, graduate led workforce. This will almost certainly depend on whether the childcare sector views this move as being less supportive of the workforce or as valuing practitioners as professionals able to use their professional judgement.

Qualifications

The Nutbrown Review (2012) has recommended an introduction (phased) of NVQ Level 3 as a minimum for working with young children. Also included is a recommendation for at least 60 per cent of course content to be about child development. As this is introduced, and practitioners are more aware of child development, it should make it easier to spot developmentally appropriate next steps for children. In the future, as childcare becomes a profession, knowledge of child development theories, action research and graduates working with all ages of children may become the norm, even an expectation, within the sector.

Progress check

One change is the introduction of the 2-year-old check for children in England. This is a new element of the statutory requirements of the EYFS (DfE 2012b: 10). Practitioners must review the child's progress between the ages of 2 and 3, producing a short written summary of progress in the prime areas of learning and development. Practitioners should 'encourage parents and/or carers to share information from the progress check with other relevant professionals, including their health visitor, and/or a teacher' (p. 11). It would appear that the aim is to encourage health and educational professionals to collaborate and share information. This is to reduce the risk of children 'falling through the net' and not being diagnosed with problems until later on, when they may be harder to correct.

This may mean that, in the future, assessments of children aged between 2 and 3 may be completed jointly between practitioners in the setting and the health visitor for the child. This would reduce the risk of parents and carers not handing on information or of information being misinterpreted. The natural progression from this would seem to be the creation of a multidiscipline practitioner who works in settings with vulnerable 2-year-olds (who are more likely to require a health visitor's intervention; Allen 2011). This may be a welcome career opportunity for those practitioners who have a particular interest or background in children's health.

Special educational needs

As the SEN legislation (DfE 2012c) is updated, it should become easier for parents to access funding for their children with SEN and to be able to choose a range of settings to suit their needs. In the future this may mean that children with SEN will access more than one setting more easily, so there will need to be more robust collaboration between settings. It may also mean that an increased number of settings will have children with SEN. With more familiarity of SEN, observations and assessments should become more commonplace and easier to do.

Technology

As technology progresses at an ever-faster rate, the way we share information with parents and carers (and children) may change in the future. Instead of written observations, there may be a short video clip, narrated by the key person, which builds into a visual biography of the child's time at the setting. This could be shared instantaneously with parents or carers, health professionals and teachers. Instead of painstakingly writing down each speech sound, the speech and language therapist could hear for herself or himself the child's exact utterances; the physiotherapist could see the progress being made in walking and the autistic spectrum specialist could spot the tiny trigger that preceded a child's distress. The observations could be translated into next steps and recorded as verbal plans, displayed on a touch screen. The practitioner simply touches the screen for the day and time, and the key person, in a message recorded that morning, explains the planned resources, rationale and suggested target children.

Key learning points

Applying the cycle of observation, assessment and planning to practice in a setting is a very effective way of supporting all areas of children's learning and development. It supports personalized provision and keeps the child at the heart of good practice. There may be many changes in the future, some predictable, some that may be a complete surprise. No matter what the changes may be, the practitioner's ability to observe, assess and plan will always be an essential core skill.

Reflective questions

1 How do you view professionalism? Consider:
   - Is professionalism only about qualifications?
   - How do qualifications support professionalism?
   - How do parents and carers view professionalism in the early years?
2 Should there be a category of 'special educational needs'? Consider:
   - All children have individual, and arguably, 'special' needs. Is SEN just another part of this continuum?
   - How do gifted and talented children differ from children with an SEN?
   - How might the social model, rather than the medical model, of SEN improve the outcomes for children and families?
3 What one piece of future technology could help you most in your role? Consider:
   - the impact on the children's learning and development;
   - communicating with parents, carers, multi-agency professionals and Ofsted;
   - could it remove your role altogether?

Further reading

Osgood, J. (2009) Childcare workforce reform in England and 'the early years professional': a critical discourse analysis, *Journal of Education Policy*, 24(6): 733–51.
Dr Osgood examines early childhood education and care (ECEC) through a political lens, and questions whether government policies are truly based on research or whether the reforms have been self-serving – 'The tidal wave of policy reform in ECEC is not founded upon objective common sense but instead stem from particular political motivations' (p. 746). It is a fascinating analysis of recent policy decisions, including the rhetoric used by successive governments, and how this shines a particular light on the 'nursery worker'.

Hatch, J.A. (2010) Rethinking the relationship between learning and development: teaching for learning in early childhood classrooms, *The Educational Forum*, 74(3): 258–68.
This article starts with a number of intriguing questions:

- What if the early childhood education field's emphasis on Jean Piaget's understandings of cognitive development turns out to be misplaced?
- What if young children are capable of complex cognitive processing that has been assumed to be impossible by mainstream early childhood educators (p. 258)?

Hatch challenges the idea that academic 'achievement' does not equate to learning with older children and should not (can not?) be applied to early childhood education. He states 'I think it is time for the early childhood field to unpack its assumptions about the relationship between development and learning' (p. 260). It is an interesting point of view, where Piaget is compared to Vygotsky and their theories are applied to modern day learning in early childhood education.

Bibliography

Allen, G. (2011) *Early Intervention: The Next Steps.* An Independent Report to Her Majesty's Government.
http://www.dwp.gov.uk/docs/early-intervention-next-steps.pdf (accessed 13 November 2012).

Appleby, K. (2010) Reflective thinking; reflective practice, in M. Reed and N. Canning (eds) *Reflective Practice in the Early Years.* London: Sage.

Aries, P. (1962) *Centuries of Childhood: A Social History of Family Life.* New York: Vintage Books.

Arnold, C. (2010) *Understanding Schemas and Emotion in Early Childhood.* London: Sage.

Assessment Reform Group (2002) *Assessment for Learning: 10 Principles. Research-based Principles to Guide Classroom Practice.*
http://www.assessment-reform-group.org/CIE3.PDF (accessed 18 November 2012).

Athey, C. (1990) *Extending Thought in Young Children: A Parent–Teacher Partnership.* London: PCP.

Ayres, J. and Robbins, J. (2005) *Sensory Integration and the Child: Understanding Hidden Sensory Challenges.* Los Angele, CA: Western Psychological Services.

Bandura, A. (1977) *Social Learning Theory.* New York: General Learning Press.

Bartholomew, L. and Bruce, T. (1993) *Getting to Know You: Record Keeping in the Early Years,* 2nd edn. London: Hodder & Stoughton Educational.

Black, P., Harrison, C., Lee, C., Marshall, B. and Wiliam, I (2003) *Assessment for Learning: Putting it into Practice.* Maidenhead: Open University Press.

Blaiklock, K. (2008) A critique of the use of Learning Stories to assess the learning dispositions of young children in New Zealand, *Research in Early Childhood Education,* 11: 77–87.
http://unitec.researchbank.ac.nz/handle/10652/1768 (accessed 28 June 2012).

Bloom, B. (ed.) (1956) *Taxonomy of Educational Objectives, The Classification of Educational Goals – Handbook I: Cognitive Domain.* New York: McKay.

Bowlby, J. (1983) *Attachment and Loss, Volume 1,* 2nd edn. New York: Basic Books.

Broadhead, P. (2006) Developing an understanding of young children's learning through play: the place of observation, interaction and reflection, *British Educational Research Journal*, 32(2): 191–207.

Bronfenbrenner, U. (1979) *The Ecology of Human Development: Experiments by Nature and Design*. Cambridge, MA: Harvard University Press.

Brooker, L., Rogers, S., Ellis, D., Hallet, E. and Roberts-Holmes, G. (2010) *Practitioners' Experience of the Early Years Foundation Stage*. Research Report DFE-RR029. London: DfE.

Bruce, T. (2005) *Early Childhood Education*, 3rd edn. London: Hodder Arnold.

Buzan, T. and Buzan, B. (1995) *The Mind Map Book: Radiant Thinking – Major Evolution in Human Thought*. Harlow: BBC Books.

Campbell-Barr, V., Lavelle, M. and Wickett, K. (2012) Exploring alternative approaches to child outcome assessments in Children's Centres, *Early Child Development and Care*, 182(7): 859–74.

Carle, E. (1996) *The Very Busy Spider*. London: Puffin.

Carr, M. (2001) *Assessment in Early Childhood Settings: Learning Stories*. London: Sage.

Carter, M. (2010) *Using 'Learning Stories' to Strengthen Teachers' Relationships with Children*. http://www.ecetrainers.com/sites/default/files/Using%20Learning%20Stories%20to%20Strengthen%20Teacher%20Relationships.pdf (accessed 13 November 2012).

Clarke, J. (2007) *Sustaining Shared Thinking*. London: A&C Black Publishers Ltd.

Clough, P. and Nutbrown, C. (2007) *A Student's Guide to Methodology*, 2nd edn. London: Sage.

Coates, D., Shimmin, A. and Thompson, W. (2009) Identifying and supporting gifted children in a nursery school (kindergarten), *Gifted Education International*, 25: 22–35.

Cohen, L., Manion, L. and Morrison, K. (2007) *Research Methods in Education*, 6th edn. London: RoutledgeFalmer.

Csikszentmihalyi, M. (2002) *Flow: The Psychology of Happiness: The Classic Work on How to Achieve Happiness*. London: Rider, Random House Group.

Curtis, A. and O'Hagan, M. (2003) *Care and Education in Early Childhood*. London: RoutledgeFalmer.

David, T., Goouch, K. and Powell, S. (2005) Research matters, in L. Abbott and A. Langston (eds) *Birth to Three Matters: Supporting the Framework of Effective Practice*. Maidenhead: Open University Press.

David, T., Goouch, K., Powell, S. and Abbott, L. (2003) *Birth to Three Matters: A Review of the Literature Compiled to Inform The Framework to Support Children in their Earliest Years*, Research Report RR444. Nottingham: DfES.

Denscombe, M. (2007) *The Good Research Guide: For Small-scale Social Research Projects*. Buckingham: Open University Press.

DCSF (Department for Children, Schools and Families) (2008a) *Every Child a Talker* Nottingham: DCSF Publications. https://www.education.gov.uk/publications/eOrderingDownload/DCSF-00854-2008.pdf (accessed 1 July 2012).

DCSF (2008b) *Letters and Sounds*. Nottingham: DCSF Publications. https://www.education.gov.uk/publications/standard/publication Detail/Page1/DCSF-00113-2008 (accessed 1 July 2012).

DCSF (2008c) *Practice Guidance for the Early Years Foundation Stage*. Nottingham: DCSF Publications.

DCSF (2010) *Challenging Practice to Further Improve Learning, Playing and Interacting in the Early Years Foundation Stage*. Nottingham: DCSF Publications.

DfE (Department for Education) (2012a) *Evaluation Schedule for Inspections of Registered Early Years Provision*. Reference no: 120086. http://www.ofsted.gov.uk/resources/using-early-years-evaluation-schedule-guidance-for-inspectors-of-registered-early-years-settings-req (accessed 13 November 2012).

DfE (Department for Education) (2012b) *Statutory Framework for the Early Years Foundation Stage*. http://media.education.gov.uk/assets/files/pdf/e/eyfs%20statutory%20framework%20march%202012.pdf (accessed 18 November 2012).

DfE (Department for Education) (2012c) *Support and Aspiration: Progress and Next Steps*. https://www.education.gov.uk/publications/standard/publication Detail/Page1/DFE-00046-2012#downloadableparts (accessed 13 November 2012).

DfES (Department for Education and Skills) (2002) *Birth to Three Matters: A Framework to Support Children in their Earliest Years*. London: DfES Publications.

DfES (2003a) *Full Day Care: National Standards for Under 8s Day Care and Childminding*. Nottingham: DfES publications.

DfES (2003b) *Every Child Matters*. London: DfES Publications.

DfES (2007) *Creating the Picture*. Norwich: OPSI.

DfES (2008) *Early Years Foundation Stage – Everything You Need to Know*. https://www.education.gov.uk/publications/eOrderingDownload/EYFS_Media_Pack.PDF (accessed 13 November 2012).

Desforges, C. with Abouchaar, A. (2003) *The Impact of Parental Involvement, Parental Support and Family Education on Pupil Achievements and Adjustment: A Literature Review*, Research Report RR433. Nottingham: DfES.

Dewey, J. (1910) *How We Think*. Lexington, MA: D.C. Heath.

Dowling, M. (2010) *Young Children's Personal, Social and Emotional Development,* 3rd edn. London: Sage.

Drifte, C. (2010) *The Manual for the Early Years SENCO.* London: Sage.

Drummond, T. (2010) *Learning Stories: Conventions for Writing.* http://earlylearningstories.info/ (accessed 28 June 2012).

Dunn, L.M., Whetton, C. and Burley, J. (1997) *The British Picture Vocabulary Scales,* 2nd edn. Windsor: NFER-Nelson.

Dunphy, E. (2010) Assessing early learning through formative assessment: key issues and considerations, *Irish Educational Studies,* 29(1): 41–56.

Dyer, M. and Taylor, S. (2012) Supporting professional identity in undergraduate Early Years students through reflective practice, *Reflective Practice: International and Multidisciplinary Perspectives,* 13(4): 551–63.

Early Education (2012) *Development Matters in the Early Years Foundation Stage* (EYFS). London: Early Education.

Edwards, C., Gandini, L. and Forman, G. (2012) *The Hundred Languages of Children: The Reggio Emilia Experience in Transformation,* 3rd edn. Santa Barbara, CA: Praeger.

Elfer, P. and Dearnley, K. (2007) Nurseries and emotional well being: evaluating an emotionally containing model of continuing professional development, *Early Years: Journal of International Research and Development,* 27(3): 267–79.

Elfer, P., Goldschmied, E. and Selleck, D. (2003) *Key Persons in the Nursery: Building Quality Relationships for Quality Provision.* London: David Fulton.

Fawcett, M. (1996) *Learning Through Child Observations.* London: Jessica Kingsley Publishers.

Featherstone, S., Beswick, C., Louis, S., Hayes, L. and Magraw, L. (2008) *Again! Again! Understanding Schemas in Young Children.* London: A&C Black Publishing Ltd.

Garvey, D. and Lancaster, A. (2010) *Leadership for Quality in Early Years and Playwork.* London: NCB.

Gindis, B. (1999) Vygotsky's vision: reshaping the practice of special education for the 21st century, *Remedial and Special Education,* 20(6): 32–64.

Grace, C. (2001) *Assessing Young Children.* http://www.pbs.org/teachers/earlychildhood/articles/assessing.html (accessed 29 June 2012).

Gray, C. and MacBlain, S. (2012) *Learning Theories in Childhood.* London: Sage.

Grenier, J. (2009) *Susan Isaacs: A Life Freeing the Minds of Children.* http://juliangrenier.blogspot.co.uk/2009/10/susan-isaacs.html (accessed 13 November 2012).

Grieshaber, S. and MacArdle, F. (2010) *The Trouble with Play.* Maidenhead: Open University Press.

Guddemi, M. and Chase, B. (2004) *Assessing Young Children*. San Antonio, TX: Pearoon Education.

Hall, J. (2005) *A Review of the Contribution of Brain Science to Teaching and Learning Neuroscience and Education*. Glasgow: The Scottish Council for Research in Education.

Hall, K., Cunneen, M., Murphy, R. et al. (2010) *Loris Malaguzzi and the Reggio Emilia Experience*. London: Continuum International Publishing Group.

Harkin, J. (2005) Fragments stored against my ruin: the place of educational theory in the professional development of teachers in further education, *Journal of Vocational Education and Training*, 57(2): 165–80.

Harwood, D., Klopper, A., Osanyin, A. and Vanderlee, M. (2012) 'It's more than care': early childhood educators' concepts of professionalism, *Early Years:* 1–14.
http://www.tandfonline.com/doi/abs/10.1080/09575146.2012.667394 (accessed 18 November 2012).

Hatch, J.A. (2010) Rethinking the relationship between learning and development: teaching for learning in early childhood classrooms, *The Educational Forum*, 74(3): 258–68.

HighScope (2012) *All about Highscope*.
http://www.highscope.org/Content.asp?ContentId=291 (accessed 13 November 2012).

Hill, S. (2009) *Learning Stories*.
http://ceparralibrary.blogspot.co.uk/2009/09/learning-stories-narrative-assessment.html (accessed 28 June 2012).

Holland, P. (2003) *We Don't Play with Guns Here*. Maidenhead: Open University Press.

Home Office (2012) *Equality Act 2010*.
http://www.homeoffice.gov.uk/equalities/equality-act/ (accessed 18 November 2012).

Hutchin, V. (1996) *Tracking Significant Achievement in the Early Years*. London: Hodder & Stoughton.

Hutchin, V. (1999) *Right from the Start: Effective Planning and Assessment in the Early Years*. London: Hodder Murray.

Hutchin, V. (2000) *Tracking Significant Achievement in the Early Years*, 2nd edn. London: Hodder Murray.

Hutchin, V. (2003) *Observing and Assessing for the Foundation Stage Profile*. London: Hodder Murray.

Hutchin, V. (2007) *Supporting Every Child's Learning Across the Early Years Foundation Stage*. London: Hodder Education.

Hutchin, V. (2012a) *Assessing and Supporting Young Children's Learning: For the Early Years Foundation Stage Profile*. London: Hodder Education.

Hutchin, V. (2012b) *The EYFS: A Practical Guide for Students and Professionals*. London: Hodder Education.

Ingleby, E. and Hedges, C. (2012) Exploring the continuing professional development needs of pedagogical practitioners in early years in England, *Professional Development in Education*: 1–17. http://www.tandfonline.com/doi/abs/10.1080.19415257.2011.651777 (accessed 18 November 2012).

Isaacs, S. (1930) *Intellectual Growth in Young Children*. London: Routledge.

Jones, A. (2005) *Montessori Education in America: An Analysis of Research Conducted from 2000–2005*. http://www.plan4preschool.org/docs/single/montessori-education-in-americaan-analysis-of-research-conducted-from-2000/ (accessed 13 November 2012).

Jones, K. (1972) *A History of the Mental Health Services*. London: Routledge.

Katz, L. and Chard, S. (2000) *Engaging Children's Minds: A Project Approach*, 2nd edn. Stamford, CT: Ablex Publishing Corporation.

Kim, Y., Sugawara, A. and Kim, G. (2000) Parents' perception of and satisfaction with the eligibility assessment of their children with special needs, *Early Child Development and Care*, 160(1): 133–42.

Kitano, S. (2011) Current issues in assessment in early childhood care and education in Japan, *Early Child Development and Care*, 181(2): 181–87.

Kolb, D. (1984) *Experiential Learning Experience as a Source of Learning and Development*. Englewood Cliffs, NJ: Prentice-Hall.

Koshy, V. and Pascal, C. (2011) Nurturing the young shoots of talent: using action research for exploration and theory building, *European Early Childhood Education Research Journal*, 19(4): 433–50.

Lindon, J. (2008) Child-initiated learning: what does it mean?, in S. Featherstone (ed.) *Like Bees, Not Butterflies: Child-initiated Learning in the Early Years*. London: A&C Black Publishers Ltd.

Lindon, J. (2010) *Reflective Practice and Early Years Professionalism*. London: Hodder Education.

Luft, J. and Ingham, H. (1950) The Johari window, a graphic model of interpersonal awareness. *Proceedings of the Western Training Laboratory in Group Development*. Los Angeles: UCLA.

Mason, C. (1923) *Towards A Philosophy of Education*, Volume 6 of the Charlotte Mason Series.

Maynard, T., Waters, J. and Clement, J. (2011) Moving outdoors: further explorations of 'child-initiated' learning in the outdoor environment. *Education 3–13, International Journal of Primary, Elementary and Early Years Education*, 1–18. http://tandfonline.com/doi/abs/10.1080/03004279.2011.578750 (accessed 18 November 2012).

McMillan, M. (2009) *The Nursery School*. Charleston, SC: Bibliobazaar.

Merrell, K. (2003) *Behavioral, Social, and Emotional Assessment of Children and Adolescents*. Hillsdale, NJ: Lawrence Erlbaum Associates Inc.

Miller, L. and Pound, L. (2011) *Theories and Approaches to Learning in the Early Years*. London: Sage.

Montessori Education (2012) *Planning*.
http://www.montessorieducationuk.org/?q=eyfs/enabling-environments/observation-assessment-and-planning/planning (accessed 13 November 2012).

Montessori, M. (1949) *The Absorbent Mind*. Oxford: Clio Press Ltd.

Montessori, M. (1965) *Dr. Montessori's Own Handbook*. New York: Schocken Books.

Moon, J. (2008) *Critical Thinking: An Exploration of Theory and Practice*. Oxford: Routledge.

Mooney, C. (2000) *Theories of Childhood: An Introduction to Dewey, Montessori, Erikson, Piaget and Vygotsky*. St Paul, MN: Redleaf Press.

Morton, K. (2012) Childcare costs parents as much as mortgage, *Nursery World*.
http://www.nurseryworld.co.uk/news/1138097/Childcare-costs-parents-mortgage/ (accessed 13 November 2012).

Moyles, J. (2008) Empowering children and adults, in S. Featherstone (ed.) *Like Bees, Not Butterflies: Child-initiated Learning in the Early Years*. London: A&C Black Publishers Ltd.

Mukherji, P. and Albon, D. (2010) *Research Methods in Early Childhood*. London: Sage.

National Strategies (2010) *Finding and Exploring Young Children's Fascinations: Strengthening the Quality of Gifted and Talented Provision in the Early Years*. Nottingham: DCSF Publications.

NCB (National Children's Bureau) (2007) PEAL project. Available at http://peal.org.uk/ (accessed 28 June 2012).

Nutbrown, C. and Page, J. (2008) *Working with Babies and Children: From Birth to Three*. London: Sage.

Nutbrown, C. (1996) *Children's Rights and Early Education*. London: Paul Chapman Publishing.

Nutbrown, C. (2006) *Threads of Thinking*, 3rd edn. London: Sage.

Nutbrown, C. and Clough, P. (2006) *Inclusion in the Early Years: Critical Analyses and Enabling Narratives*. London: Sage.

Nutbrown, C., Clough, P. and Selbie, P. (2008) *Early Childhood Education: History, Philosophy and Experience*. London: Sage.

Nutbrown Review (2012) *Foundations for Quality: The Independent Review of Early Education and Childcare Qualifications*.
http://www.education.gov.uk/nutbrownreview (accessed 13 November 2012).

O'Brien, N. and Moules, T. (2007) So round the spiral again: a reflective participatory research project with children and young people, *Educational Action Research,* 15(3): 385–402.

Ofsted (2012) *Evaluation Schedule for Inspections of Registered Early Years Provision.* Manchester: Ofsted Publications.

Osgood, J. (2009) Childcare workforce reform in England and 'the early years professional': a critical discourse analysis, *Journal of Education Policy,* 24(6): 733–51.

Paige-Smith, A. and Craft, A. (eds) (2007) *Developing Reflective Practice in the Early Years.* Maidenhead: Open University Press.

Palaiologou, I. (ed.) (2010) Policy context in England and the implementation of the Early Years Foundation Stage, in I. Palaiologou (ed.) *The Early Years Foundation Stage: Theory and Practice.* London: Sage.

Perry, B. and Szalavitz, M. (2008) *The Boy Who Was Raised as a Dog.* New York: Basic Books.

Piaget, J. and Inhelder, B. (1969) *The Psychology of the Child.* New York: Basic Books.

Podmore, V. and Carr, M. (1999) Learning and teaching stories: new approaches to assessment and evaluation. Paper presented at the AARE - NZARE Conference on Research in Education, Melbourne, 1 December.

Polanyi, M. (1966) The *Tacit Dimension.* London: Routledge.

Pound, L. (2005) *How Children Learn.* London: Step Forward Publishing Ltd.

Powell, M. and Smith, A. (2006) Ethical guidelines for research with children: a review of current research ethics documentation in New Zealand, Kotuitui, *New Zealand Journal of Social Sciences,* 1(2): 125–38.

Pugh, G. (2010) *Principles for Engaging with Families: A Framework for Local Authorities and National Organisations to Evaluate and Improve Engagement with Families.* London: NCB.

QCA/DFEE (2000) *Curriculum Guidance for the Foundation Stage.* Coventry: QCA Publishing.

Reed, M. and Canning, N. (eds) (2010) *Reflective Practice in the Early Years.* London: Sage.

Riddall-Leech, S. (2003) *Managing Children's Behaviour (Professional Development).* Oxford: Heinemann.

Riddall-Leech, S. (2008) *How to Observe Children,* 2nd edn. London: Heinemann.

Roberts, C. (2011) Supporting development, *Make the Grade: The Journal of the Chartered Institute of Educational Assessors,* Summer.

Roberts-Holmes, G. (2005) *Doing your Early Years Research Project.* London: Sage.

Roopnarine, J. and Johnson, J. (2008) *Approaches to Early Childhood Education.* Harlow: Pearson.

Samuelsson, I. and Sheridan, S. (2009) Preschool quality and young children's learning in Sweden, *International Journal of Child Care and Education Policy*, 3(1): 1–11.

Schiller, W. (1999) Adult/child interaction: how patterns and perceptions can influence planning, *Early Child Development and Care*, 159: 75–92.

Schön, D. (1983) *The Reflective Practitioner: How Professionals Think in Action*. New York: Basic Books.

Schrag, Z. (2011) The case against ethics review in the social sciences, *Research Ethics*, 7(4): 120–31.

Shafer, S. (2007) *Education is an Atmosphere, a Discipline, a Life: Charlotte Mason's Three-pronged Approach to Education*. Grayson, GA: Simply Charlotte Mason.

Sharman, C., Cross, W. and Vennis, D. (1995) *Observing Children*. London: Continuum.

Simpson, D. (2010) Being professional? Conceptualising early years professionalism in England, *European Early Childhood Education Research Journal*, 18(1): 5–14.

Siraj-Blatchford, I. (1996) Language, culture and difference, in C. Nutbrown (ed.) *Children's Rights and Early Education*. London: PC Publishing.

Siraj-Blatchford, I., Sylva, K., Muttock, S., Gilden, R. and Bell, D. (2002) *Researching Effective Pedagogy in the Early Years*. Norwich: DfES.

Solvason, C. (2012) Research and the early years practitioner-researcher, *Early Years: An International Journal of Research and Development*, 1–10.

Standards and Testing Agency (2012) *Assessment and Reporting Arrangements: Early Years Foundation Stage*.
http://www.aaia.org.uk/content/uploads/2010/07/assessment-and-reporting-arrangements-early-years-foundation-stage-profile.pdf (accessed 18 November 2012).

Stoll Lillard, A. (2005) *Montessori: The Science Behind the Genius*. New York: Oxford University Press.

Swaffield, S. (2011) Getting to the heart of authentic Assessment for Learning, *Assessment in Education: Principles, Policy & Practice*, 18(4): 433–49.

Sylva, K., Melhuish, E., Sammons, P., Siraj-Blatchford, I. and Taggart, B. (2004) *The Effective Provision of Pre-School Education [EPPE] Project: A Longitudinal Study funded by the DfES 1997–2004*. London: DfES.

Sylva, K., Melhuish, E., Sammons, P., Siraj-Blatchford, I. and Taggart, B. (2010) *Early Childhood Matters*. London: Routledge.

Tannenbaum, F. (1938) *Crime and Community*. London: Columbia University Press.

Tickell, C. (2011) *The Early Years: Foundations for Life, Health and Learning*. An Independent Report on the Early Years Foundation Stage to Her Majesty's Government. London: Department for Education.

UNICEF (2012) *The Convention on the Rights of the Child.*
http://www.unicef.org/crc/ (accessed August 2012).

Vogt, P. and Johnson, B. (2011) *Dictionary of Statistics & Methodology.*
London: Sage.

Vygotsky, L. (1962) *Thought and Language.* Cambridge, MA: MIT Press.

Vygotsky, L. (1978) *Mind in Society.* Cambridge, MA: Harvard University
Press.

Wall, K. (2011) *Special Needs and Early Years.* London: Sage.

Warash, B., Curtis, R., Hursh, D. and Tucci, V. (2008) Skinner meets Piaget
on the Reggio playground: practical synthesis of applied behavior
analysis and developmentally appropriate practice orientations, *Journal of Research in Childhood Education,* 22(4): 441–53.

Warnock, M. (1978) *Special Educational Needs: The Warnock Report.* London: HMSO.

Watt, D. (2007) On becoming a qualitative researcher: the value of reflexivity, *The Qualitative Report,* 12(1): 82–101.

Weston, P. (1998) *Friedrich Froebel: His Life, Times and Significance.*
London: Roehampton Institute.

Wexler-Sherman, C., Gardner, H. and Feldman, D. (1988) A pluralistic
view of early assessment: the project spectrum approach, *Theory Into Practice,* 27(1): 77–83.

Whalley, M. (2007) *Involving Parents in their Children's Learning.* London:
Sage.

White, J. (2008) *Playing and Learning Outdoors.* London: Routledge.

Whitehead, M. (2004) *Language and Literacy in the Early Years,* 3rd edn.
London: Sage.

Wilkin, A., Derrington, C., White, R. et al. (2010) *Improving the Outcomes for Gypsy, Roma and Traveller Pupils.*
https://www.education.gov.uk/publications/RSG/AllRsgPublications/
Page11/DFE-RR043 (accessed 18 November 2012).

Williams, P. (2008) *Independent Review of Mathematics Teaching in Early Years Settings and Primary Schools.* Nottingham: DCSF.

Woodrow, C. (2008) Discourses of professional identity in early childhood: movements in Australia, *European Early Childhood Education Research Journal,* 16(2): 269–80.

Worthington, M. and Carruthers, E. (2003) Research uncovers children's
creative mathematical thinking, *Primary Mathematics,* 7(3): 21–5.

Zastrow, C. and Kirst-Ashman, K. (2010) *Understanding Human Behavior and the Social Environment.* Belmont, CA: Brooks/Cole.

Index